How to Thrive Abroad

Life Lessons from Living in Denmark

MIHAELA MIHOVA

Illustrations by C'MNKY Art

Copenhagen, 2017

MIHAELA MIHOVA

HOW TO THRIVE ABROAD

First published in Copenhagen, Denmark 2017

Copyright © Mihaela Mihova

Edited by Cornerstones Literary Consultancy, London UK 2016

Illustrations by C'MNKY Art, Copenhagen (Instagram @c.mnky)

Cover photo by photographer Villi Pefticheva

All other tables, figures, pictures and graphs by Mihaela Mihova

ISBN 978-87-970040-0-5

Creative Non-Fiction

All rights reserved. No part of this publication may be reproduced, stored in a retrieval system, or transmitted, in any form, or by any means (electronic, mechanical, photocopying, recording or otherwise) without the prior written permission of the author.

This book is sold subject to the condition that it shall not, by way of trade or otherwise, be lent, hired out, or otherwise circulated without the author and publisher's prior consent in any form of binding or cover other than in that in which it is published and without a similar condition including the condition being imposed on the subsequent purchaser.

The stories in this book reflect the author's recollection of events. Some names and identifying characteristics have been changed to protect the privacy of those depicted. Dialogue has been re-created from memory.

'I recommend this book to everyone who is considering to study abroad. I wish I had this book before I went to Denmark for my studies. Besides the experiences Mihaela shares about her life as an expatriate, her book has truly inspirational insights on personal development that will help future students to thrive abroad.'

- *Sandra Dorn, Management Consultant*

'*How to Thrive Abroad* is a MUST for anyone living abroad or considering embarking on such journey, and can save you a lot of headaches on the inevitable emotional rollercoaster. In a profound, powerful and heart-warming approach - Mihaela lead us through her story with inspiring lessons anyone can relate to.'

- *Stoyan Yankov, Keynote Speaker, Entrepreneur and Movie Producer*

'With this book Mihaela shares a rare insight into the personal story of a global citizen. I am sure her story will be an inspiration to future and current international students, and help them thrive abroad.'

- *Jane Midtgaard, Career Consultant at Aarhus BSS Career & Alumni, Aarhus BSS, Aarhus University*

'Luck does not come for free! Learn hands-on strategies on how to navigate in the complex Danish culture. *How to Thrive Abroad* is based on Mihaela's own experiences since the day she had arrived in Denmark as an 18 years old girl from Bulgaria.'

- Jakob Boman, Founder at BOOKANAUT, Management Consultant and Entrepreneur

About the author

Mihaela, or Misha as her friends and family call her, is an author from Bulgaria living in Copenhagen, Denmark. Since 2009, she has been studying and working abroad, due to a strong professional interest in working internationally. She holds a Master's degree in Business and Economics from Aarhus University (Denmark) and has been working within Business Development for global Danish and international companies. Mihaela is also a writer, athlete, entrepreneur, dancer, and blogger, a girl with an open and curious mind, and adventurous spirit.

In her spare time, Mihaela is a goodwill ambassador for anti-discrimination and human rights at the United Nations Youth Association (UNYA) of Denmark, where she is driving projects in cooperation with UN affiliates.

She has been a guest speaker at career events for international students in Denmark and abroad, as well as a former mentor for foreign business graduates at Aarhus University. Presently, she is also part of the Scandinavian talents network NOVA.

Before moving to Denmark, Mihaela has been a professional athlete for 10 years in competitive ballroom dancing and is now a fitness and sports aficionado.

The author is in love with Copenhagen, but whenever she takes time off, she is on the road, torn between travelling back to Bulgaria to visit her family, and travelling the world with her boyfriend.

This is her first novel.

Visit Mihaela's website www.mihaelamihova.net to read related blog posts, to find features, and to learn about future releases.

Get in touch with Mihaela:

Instagram:
@misha.mihova
Author Facebook page:
https://www.facebook.com/mihaelageorgievamihova/
LinkedIn:
www.linkedin.com/in/mihaelageorgievamihova

To my mother and father,

for their unconditional love and support,

for being the brightest people and best role models in the world,

for giving me the freedom to dream, achieve, and fly away

Contents

About the author

Introduction 1

PART ONE: GETTING TO KNOW A NEW WORLD 9

    Chapter One – A New Beginning 9

    Chapter Two – Drive 25

    Chapter Three – Reality-Check 36

    Chapter Four – Breaking the Room of Glass 61

    Chapter Five – The Local Habits 75

PART TWO: MAKING THINGS HAPPEN 93

    Chapter Six – Practices of 'Going Further' 93

        Outside-In Approach – creating a vision 96

        Practice 1. List your achievements for a definite period 96

        Practice 2. Prepare a list of the things you would like to do, or do not understand 101

        Practice 3. Make a 'Dreams Plan' for Long-term Goals 111

        Inside-Out Approach – when you have a clear vision and would like to achieve it 124

        Practice 1. Identify Main Values 125

        Practice 2. Identify 'Key Factors for Success' 130

        Practice 3. Identify (Additional) Resources 135

        What if things are still not happening? 137

    Chapter Seven – International Career Part 1 141

        Lesson 1. Self-discovery is the prerequisite for setting a direction 143

Lesson 2. Take your life mantras with a grain of salt 153

Lesson 3. The world is 'slowly getting there' 162

Chapter Eight – International Career Part 2 167

Lesson 1. Preparation is everything – show your motivation and know how to present yourself 167

Lesson 2. Proactivity and Passion win over Passiveness 181

Lesson 3. Find a problem you care about and start solving it 186

Wrap-up 190

PART THREE: THE SHAPE OF THE MULTINATIONAL LIFE 195

Chapter Nine – Finding the Right Place 195

Chapter Ten – Ten Things I Wish I had Known Before I Moved Abroad 204

Chapter Eleven – The Sky Over Home 219

References and Suggested Books for Inspiration 237

Acknowledgements 238

Introduction

The purpose of this book is not to help you survive, but to push you to thrive and succeed.

What does it take to pursue an international degree abroad, have a global career, and live a multicultural life?

The life abroad is colorful and multi-dimensional. If I had to use only one word to describe it, I would choose 'overwhelming' – because of the complete change of reality that must be absorbed. I have learned this from firsthand experience, when I left the beautiful country of Bulgaria on an international journey towards Denmark, which started in 2009. I was then at the young age of eighteen, and in pursuit of my goal to have a higher education at one of the top universities in the world, and to experience what it was like to live abroad and see the world.

Looking back at the past seven years of living abroad, I do not believe that the labels 'expatriate', 'foreigner', 'immigrant' or 'international student/employee' fit my reality. For example, even though I use the term often throughout the book as an easy reference, I cannot define myself as an expatriate. 'Expatriate' refers to a person, who is on a short-term (usually up to two years) contract abroad, typically work- or project-related. During my time at business school, I specialized in

International Business, which, as the name of the programme suggests, focused on all aspects of doing business globally, including the life of expatriates. When we talked about expatriation, we always referred to the short-term 'assignments' and need for repatriation when the expatriates return home.

Expatriates are believed by the international management literature and research not to blend into the local community. This is due to the nature of their assignments and because they usually have corporate support behind them, and do not go through the struggle that self-initiated expatriates or international students do. Expatriates are supported by their companies with monetary compensation, accommodation and transportation. Moreover, they are often believed to live in closed societies together with other expatriates. This is perhaps partly because they do not see the need to be too integrated in their host countries. Of course, these are general facts and there are many exceptions. Expatriates are believed to be mainly concentrated on completing the 'special mission' for which they have been sent – and the company 'at home' often takes care of their life abroad.

Therefore, based on the above definition, I do not fall into the expatriate group, as I moved to Denmark on my own terms, and to pursue an education.

Introduction

Looking at the 'foreigner' and 'immigrant' labels, after all I have read and heard, I can conclude with bitterness that these are somehow often looked at with a negative slant. The word 'foreign' is typically linked to the unknown, the different, the complicated and the risky. After living in Denmark for over five years, I no longer saw myself as a foreigner. Probably my integration within Denmark has been easier considering that I was born and raised in Bulgaria. I suppose that being European predisposes one for some shared dimensions such as geography, economic conditions, membership in the European Union and more, leading to a relatively low 'psychic distance'.[1]

The term 'immigrant' is then generally used for people who pursue jobs abroad. Refugees who are seeking asylum are also regarded as immigrants.

Even though I have been working (student jobs, internships, projects, own ventures and then a full-time job) the entire time I have been living in Denmark, my purpose when I relocated was to gain a university education abroad. I was referred to as an 'international student' by the university when I applied to the programme in 2009, which of course I can completely relate to, as the admission

---

[1] In the International Business (IB) literature, psychic distance is described as the perceived distance between two countries. It is often measured by the CAGE (Cultural, Administrative, Geographical and Economic) factors that influence the perception of distance between countries, introduced by Professor Pankaj Ghemawat.

requirements were different for local applicants than for students from abroad. Regardless of that, for the rest of my studies, and until the very day of graduation, we were not divided into internationals and locals (students from Denmark) by the university – we were all one group, studying under the same rules, requirements and study regulations.

What is left, then, for me? A Bulgarian in Denmark? Where do I fit? I am not an expatriate, I am not a Dane, but neither am I a foreigner, as I have been living abroad for long enough that my cultural identity has become very mixed.

I believe the answer is a *global citizen* with international cultural identity. Can you relate?

My journey has taught me that once you get down 'that road' of international living and development, there is no coming back – mindset-wise and identity-wise. I have learned that being a global citizen means living on constant crossroads. Quite a unique and exciting place to be, but at times also very frustrating. Even when you have settled in your new 'home' country, you still face nostalgia for your homeland, while another part of you – the one that has kicked you out of your comfort zone into a 'country far, far away' – demands that you stay open for new adventures. However, even if you are open-minded, the new reality around you can trigger disappointment when meeting biased people – those that are bound to prejudices, risk-

Introduction

averseness and poor judgment. You should learn to look beyond that. What does the road ahead look like?

I decided to write this book because of countless emails and contacts I have been receiving from people, most of them international students or young professionals abroad, who have been trying to 'find their way' in a new country, and are searching for advice, tips on life abroad, and firsthand experience – just as I was in 2009.

The questions and topics of the people who have reached out to me cover a wide range of concerns. Some of them are: What is it like to have a long-distance relationship? What is it like to study abroad? What does it take to pursue a career abroad and to thrive in a multinational environment? Did you experience culture shock and what was it like? How do you cope with culture shock? How is it to speak foreign languages every day, to adapt to a new culture, to live and develop, personally and professionally abroad? What are the advantages of being a foreigner when you pursue a career abroad? What are the impressions, experiences and lessons you have gained from the past several years of studying and working abroad?

These and many other questions have inspired me to write this book with the hope that it will give you interesting and inspirational perspectives on all the above and much more. 'I have been there' and I would like to help you succeed – by making your life abroad easier. I must add that this book will not solve all dilemmas. However, the book is a synthesized, brief but concrete reflection of the most important lessons I have learned from living abroad. The story covers the things that I wished I had known before leaving my home country, and diving head over heels into my life as an international student. You do not have to use everything you find in this book – but instead, select the things that you believe can be valuable for you.

I realized that if I had so many questions and doubts to which I had difficulty finding the answers before studying abroad, and if so many other people seem to have the same concerns, then there must be thousands of people around the world who feel the same way. My focus therefore has been on how to help these people, on a much larger scale. Sharing my experience and lessons learned so far is one of my commitments to helping young professionals achieve their goals – be it at home or abroad.

The book is divided into three parts.

The first section titled *'Part One: Getting to Know a New World'* consists of the stories at the beginning of my journey as a newly arrived international student in Denmark. It covers the initial impressions and feelings of adjusting to the new world abroad.

The second section is titled *'Part Two: Making Things Happen'* and is focused on goal-setting, personal development and pursuing an international career. Important philosophies and lessons learned are outlined as best practices based on my trial-and-error experience abroad.

The third and last part of the book named *'Part Three: The Shape of The Multinational Life'* shares the things that I wished I had known before I moved abroad. It reflects on living an international life, on the choices made as a global citizen, on finding the right place – both geographically and metaphorically, and, eventually, on finding my ground abroad.

For clear reflection on each experience I present, I have included a small epilogue after each chapter, with the key 'take away(s)' from the covered topic.

Regardless of whether you are a self-initiated expatriate, an international student or someone who dreams about an international education and/or global career, this book is for you. Whether you have already reached this crossroad in your life, are considering to pursue it, or could use the extra help and advice of how to set a course for where you want to be, this book is for you. Regardless of where you are from in the world, if you can relate to the notion of a global citizen, then you might find something useful too.

Therefore, the book is devoted to all of you who are courageously ready to follow your dreams, despite all barriers and difficulties, who are determined to explore new worlds, start new lives or make a change, and want to make a difference – today. I also sincerely hope that this book will serve as a source of inspiration for many of you to have the courage to chase after what you want.

It is therefore my pleasure to guide you through the lessons I have learned so far during my journey as an international student, foreign graduate, and then a business professional abroad. I have illustrated these lessons by means of personal stories, goal-setting tips, as well as sharing my perspectives and advice about How to Thrive Abroad.

PART ONE: GETTING TO KNOW A NEW WORLD

First Impressions, Insights and Further Thoughts of Young Expatriate

Chapter One – A New Beginning

Far Away

I remember how the air was full of electrical density, a mix of nostalgia and anticipation. It was an end, and yet a new beginning.

I was eighteen years old, and freshly graduated from the Secondary School of Foreign Languages 'Vasil Levski'[2] in my divine coastal hometown Burgas. Just a month before, I had received an acceptance letter from my top priority university – Aarhus School of Business, Aarhus University (ASB, AU).[3] It said that I had been accepted for the Bachelor's degree of Business Administration and Economics at Aarhus University in Denmark, and I was indescribably happy – I had this feeling that all the hard work had been worth it and was about to

---

[2] Named after Bulgarian revolutionary and national hero (Apostle of Freedom). In Bulgarian: Васил Левски.
[3] The university was called Aarhus School of Business back in 2009. Since 2012, the business school has merged with Aarhus University and is now named Aarhus University, Business and Social Sciences.

pay off. Since an early age, I had longed to experience what the world had to offer outside the comfortable home-boundaries. I always dreamed of being able to make an impact on a global scale.

As much as I loved my beautiful home country, I'd always been able to picture myself studying abroad, living, growing up and developing in a multicultural environment; I adored the burning excitement in my chest brought about by the anticipation of new challenges beyond my imagination. Diversity inspired me – to learn and develop, to travel and experience; I craved to explore new places and cultures. I aspired to work with people from different backgrounds, and I dreamed about a global education and career – one without borders and limits. Despite my enthusiasm, I also had to embrace the uncertainty and the fact that my world from this day on would change completely.

It was 22 August 2009, an ordinary day for many, but for me it was the day when I was leaving for Denmark, in order to start my Introduction Week at Aarhus University, which would begin just two days later. It was the first time I would live so far away for such a long period from my family, my boyfriend and my friends: at this age, basically everyone I loved and everything I knew. The 'big' day had arrived so fast, and despite all my preparation, I still could not believe that I was going to a study in a country at the other end of Europe, for at least three years. I was leaving my home for a place, where I didn't know anyone, where

I was to be dependent only on myself, and where I didn't even have housing yet. Even though my departure felt too soon, I knew I'd been given a wonderful chance and I could not let it pass me by.

I had been glancing at the world map hung over my desk every day since receiving my acceptance letter. I was specifically looking at the small green Nordic country, 'up there' next to the Baltic Sea, which seemed so far away from the small green Southern country, located 'down there' next to the Black Sea. I knew they were less than 3000 km away from one other[4], but the distance seemed larger on the map. Then, childish as it sounds, I had always put my forefinger on Denmark and my thumb on Bulgaria, to find out that they were only a span away from each other, after all. When anxiety woke me up in the middle of the night, I could instinctively turn to the wall opposite the bed and stare at the world map. The silly thought of how my hand could capture the distance between Bulgaria and Denmark was my personal assurance, the hope and belief that everything was going to be fine.

There were only few minutes before we had to leave, and I turned one last time to look at my childhood room for a quiet goodbye. That room had witnessed my greatest achievements and humiliations throughout

---

[4] The distance between Denmark and Bulgaria is approximately 2600 km (driving), as calculated from Copenhagen to Burgas.

the past eighteen years. From learning to walk, to learning to do the perfect splits as a young dancesport competitor, to all the medals that I had brought home from competitions afterwards. It had witnessed firsthand my school lessons, learning Bulgarian, then my difficulties with complicated Russian grammar and mastering English. It had observed my constant efforts, ambitions and failures, but also my best achievements until then, the fears and dreams. The room should have learned one lesson from the past years – that efforts and determination is what it takes to succeed, and there are no short cuts to achieving goals.

My glance immediately fell on the bookshelves in my room, covered with beautiful pictures in frames – all of them received as farewell presents from my family, friends and classmates. Some of the collages were also from my teammates from the dancesport club, picturing us at competitions and concerts; other were from events with co-members from Rotary International,[5] where I was a goodwill ambassador. My world in frames.

Next to these were the framed photos of me and my classmates from high school and from our wonderful prom, as well as from the study trip to Moscow that I did in 2007. Staring at the pictures, I could not

---

[5] Rotary International is a humanitarian organization, committed to global service and humanitarian relief. It brings together bright students, business professionals and leaders to work for different causes and to bring peace around the world.

help but think that I must have been the luckiest girl on the planet to have had such wonderful moments, and family, boyfriend and friends such as these. They had all been supportive and encouraging, and I could not be happier for having them in my life, yet sadder for not being able to see them as often anymore. We looked so ridiculous and embarrassing in some pictures, but I didn't care. I couldn't believe that these people would not be around me anymore, that they wouldn't be part of my new world; that I would not share with them all the new experiences and adventures that lay ahead of me.

'Nothing can substitute you,' I promised the static versions of my friends in the pictures.

Looking at my reflection in the mirror, I tried to fix my long blonde hair into a ponytail; my eyes looked more red than blue, because of the sleepless, emotional night I'd just had. My boyfriend and I had said goodbye the afternoon before, so I could spend my last night in Burgas with my family. For the past week, I had said 'goodbye' to so many people – childhood friends, teammates, my classmates, and relatives – that I was already exhausted emotionally.

Yet, as my day of departure had approached, I knew I had to leave the most amazing boy on the planet, and back then it was the hardest thing I had ever done in my life. What frustrated me the most was that I could see how much my departure hurt him, and I felt so helpless. Long-distance relationships never work, was what everyone said.

Jasen was the first boy I had ever been in love with and, ironically, we had met during my senior year in high school, several months before this summer day when I was leaving for Denmark. I had never felt that special connection before.

When my senior year had started, I had made a promise to myself that I would not start a relationship, given that my goal was to pursue a higher education abroad. As my last year in high school was extremely overwhelming, and given the fact that I had never been in love before, I was sure that this would be the easiest promise in the world to keep.

I met Jasen when I was seventeen, at the Rotary Youth Club Interact – a humanitarian organization for students aged fourteen to eighteen, who are passionate about making a difference. I had always wanted to be part of such a goodwill organization. Since I was too young back then to join UNICEF or any other United Nations affiliate, instead I had worked with several cases in collaboration with The Red Cross and my dancesport club, where we had taken part in fund-raising dance concerts, and had organized campaigns on different humanitarian topics.

Yet when my friend Dany, who was a member of Interact, invited me to join Rotary at the beginning of my senior year, I declined firmly. Even though I knew that it was my best chance to join, since receiving recommendation by a current member was a prerequisite for that, I could not see how another extra-curriculum would fit in my overbooked senior year. The year was already highly demanding, starting with a Russian-language certificate exam, followed by a Bulgarian History exam, and then by a TOEFL English test. On top of all this, there were the two crucial final exams, whilst I had to concentrate my efforts on university applications, coupled with student jobs and sports. My rare spare time was fully devoted to spending time with my friends and family. Volunteering did not fit my tight schedule that year.

It took me only one month to change my mind, because of what I regard to be the most depressing documentary film I had ever seen in my life. It featured the life of homeless children in Moscow. I was aware that even though the film was about the children in Moscow, there were kids in similar circumstances everywhere in the world. The scenes traumatized me so much that this triggered a desperate, restless desire to take immediate action, to help these children and more around the world have better lives. And since then, I have been committed to the cause. That was why I had joined the Rotary Youth

Committee Interact in Burgas, and how one of the worst things I have seen in my life led, unintentionally, to one of my best.

The first time I met Jasen was on a rainy October day, in a small café, where we met with some of the members before my very first weekly Rotary meeting. He was confident, intelligent, self-aware and had the attitude of *I do the right thing and don't care what others think*. I recognized it immediately, because it was exactly my attitude towards most aspects of life. Jasen had a natural charm and leadership aura, which none could resist. He was one year younger than I was, but since he'd been born at the end of the calendar year, he was signed up for school a year later, which meant he was two academic years 'behind' me. Like me, he was studying in a language school and was doing sports on a professional level, while engaging in goodwill activities such as being part of Rotary. Since my everyday life was also highly proactive, I had been always fascinated by people who had the same level of energy, engagement, life dynamics and passion for sports, travel and volunteer work. I admired people who were taking the initiative to make a change. He looked athletic, composed and he was wearing his confidence lightly. I felt as if I had finally met a soul mate, someone who I could relate to.

I had waited to fall in love for so long and when it finally happened, I had to leave him behind, to live 3000 km away. Brilliant timing.

Jasen and I swiftly became close friends and I found out what it meant to be crazy about someone. We could not stay away from each other. The more I got to know him during the following months, and the more we worked together on projects, the harder it was to imagine my world without him. Be it in Bulgaria or Denmark, anywhere – my life had to have him in it. Jasen, and his honey-blond messy hair, handsome pale skin, bright brown eyes, wide shoulders, athletic body and a smile that could light up the world. 'Handsome' was a word created to describe him, I had thought, secretly staring at him during our Rotary Interact meetings. Was it fair for a person to be so perfect? To be that smart, noble, caring, funny, and to look like that? It was unfair – and I was in love.

'I am crazy about him,' I had admitted to Yana, my childhood friend, while we were chatting together at her room in Burgas over our upcoming graduation and the big soon-to-be-freshmen-at-university plans. It was simply amazing that we were seniors in high school already – and that we were going to be living apart from each other in just a couple of months. It seemed unbelievable. Yana and I had been inseparable since graduating elementary school, even though we studied in different gymnasiums.

'I am about to leave for a university miles away, and the last thing that I wanted or needed was a relationship.' Love.

'You could not have planned it, and you know how it is; things like that do not work as you expect even if they are planned.' Yana replied. I wondered how there could be any way out of it without anyone getting hurt – and there wasn't.

I remembered the first-time Yana ever met Jasen. My friend and I were travelling on a city bus when Jasen unexpectedly boarded it. *'Mish… he is just so gorgeous indeed!'* Yana whispered to me, evidently surprised, squeezing my hand approvingly while Jasen approached us. While having similar moral values, my friend and I had very different tastes in everything else in life: music, clothes, style, how we liked our coffee in the morning, study programs, career aspirations, among other aspects. Hence, as you can imagine, she had never approved of anyone I thought as attractive – even famous actors, who were generally perceived as talented and beautiful. That was something new too.

Jasen and I had spent half a year as good friends, and less than two months as boyfriend and girlfriend, before I left Bulgaria for Denmark. For these last two months, he had been just the most wonderful, caring and considerate boyfriend I could ever have imagined. Now, years later, when I think about how the circumstances around us were, I get extremely angry about how unfair life was. Sometimes you meet the right person at the wrong time and know that love is not enough. I have the urge in despair to help these two kids in love. Interesting, though, how the eighteen-year-old me never felt this way back then, and did not see the situation as 'unfair'. The younger me was so happy and 'consumed' by all the amazing and new things in her life that she did not have the energy and time to analyze what was unfair. Instead of desperation, I somehow had a calm acceptance that our relationship would be something that would need a lot of effort and nurturing.

Our goodbye was flashing back to me repeatedly, and it had been doing exactly that during the entire night before my departure. I could not let our story, which had not even begun, end like this.

My mind was a big mess of questions. When would we see each other again? What if we couldn't make it through the long-distance? There were exactly two years until he would graduate high school, and meanwhile I was going to live miles away. We were about to thrive in different worlds, and nothing could change that. Only time – if we would let it. Would we stand a chance of having any future together? *'No, of course you wouldn't,'* the inner voice of rationality inside my head reminded me. *'Some things are just not meant to be.'* I told myself. Maybe it was best to let Jasen go, let him be happy with someone else, instead of waiting for me. This seemed like a rational choice, as well as no doubt a noble act of selflessness; this was the right thing to do.

Looking back then at my life up until that moment, I realized I had never allowed myself to be selfish, despite my strong independence and self-reliance. I believed that someone was only fortunate when they shared knowledge, compassion and great empathy. I believed that people should have hearts big enough to make choices based on what was best for most people involved, not what would bring the most value for their own sake. Until the summer of 2009, when I decided that this time, I would make all my graduate choices based only on what I most wanted – not what was rationally perceived as 'right' or what others expected from me. That was how I left the comfort of home and made a completely selfish choice to not give up on our relationship.

'We are going to talk on skype whenever we can,' I'd said quietly to Jasen the day before my departure to Denmark. It was a warm, late afternoon, which I will always remember. We were standing outside my apartment building, hugging tightly, saying our goodbyes. *'We will make this work,'* I continued, reassuring myself as much as him.

Jasen nodded, leaned down and kissed me: a soft, gentle, goodbye kiss, full of promise. He and I could talk forever, about everything, but at this moment it did not feel as if we had 'forever' ahead of us, nor had we words for each other. We were running out of time, and our story was slipping away from us before it even got the chance to start.

We promised each other to turn away and not look back. After we had parted, I walked into the building entrance, and ran up the stairs to the second floor. There I stopped and stood next to the glass windows, and this was where I broke yet another promise. I turned around and stared at him walking away, wondering where all the air in this world had disappeared to. As someone who had never been in love before, I had always believed that falling in love was the hardest thing in the world. Sustaining that love turned out to be the difficult bit. It was then that I realized and believed that probably nothing would be the same again, no matter what would happen next. This was what growing apart was about to do, I was sure. I knew that next time we would meet, in four, six or nine months, we would be different people. So many things could and would affect us – situations, people that we were going to meet, the distance. We were going our own ways, and even if we managed to stay together, I feared that what we felt for each other would never again be this innocent, unconditional love we had at this moment. However, I was willing to take that risk – what if somehow, someday, we would find a way back to each other? Because there was a chance, even if a small one, that I could be wrong.

***

Change – everything was going to change in several minutes. I could feel that Change would be my inevitable companion in life, in my new world far away from home. But I was going to let it, and despite everything, I was completely thrilled by the idea of it.

After all, as I had found out, Bulgaria and Denmark were only a span away from each other.

I remember clearly how I turned around and watched my wonderful, supporting family that I loved with all my heart, preparing to leave for the airport with me. I silently thanked the Universe for having them. I knew well back then that they did not want me to go. Until the moment my plane took off from Burgas Airport, I was sure that they hoped and somehow expected that I would turn around at the last moment and say, *'Hey… you know what? I think I am actually going to stay.'*

Before I left, I noticed that the Hibiscus Chinese rose on my balcony had blossomed that same morning: it now bore three big, beautiful red flowers. It had hardly ever done that before, so it must have been a good sign, I thought, as I closed the door behind me, ready to embrace my new world.

Epilogue

Parting with the dearest people in your life and everyone you know, while diving into the unknown, could be scary, especially when you are an inexperienced eighteen-year-old, who has never been living more than 30 km away from home before.

What I know for sure is that 'scared' was not how I felt. However, I had all these mixed feelings: I was extremely excited, yet also nervous;

I was concerned whether I would manage to find a part-time student job to support my education, and I was also doubtful about whether my friendships and my long-distance relationship would last.

When it comes to the long-distance relationship, I wanted it to work out so badly that my chest literally hurt each time I thought of us being apart. Nevertheless, I could not let the chance of following my dreams pass me by, or question my decision to study abroad, which I did not doubt for a second.

Regarding the friendships, time shows you that no matter what you promise each other, the new social surroundings will influence significantly how these relationships evolve. You will all meet new people, make wonderful new friends, and move on. While some friendships will grow stronger and endure, other will change. The more you thrive in different environments, visit new places, meet new people, and share different experiences, concerns and joys, the more some of your old relationships will sadly fade over time. However, there will be other friendships that will stay the same, regardless of how much you change and how many interesting new people you meet along the way. Even if you do not talk with each other often, even if you are separated by miles, every time you meet, everything would feel the same. These friends nothing can substitute.

Embracing a completely new world is not an easy choice, but it is the best learning experience you can have. Once you've taken the road of a global citizen, you'll find you can never go back to being the same person you were before the journey. Each time now when I must be extremely courageous, I remember the eighteen-year-old girl who left a perfect and comfortable life at home to pursue her dream in a foreign country; who aspired to achieve new and challenging endeavours with determination and persistency, and managed to build everything from scratch. If I could do it then, so I can now.

Chapter Two – Drive

Out of the Comfort Zone

I had always found the bird's eye view from the plane stunning. The sight of the cottonwool clouds underneath the sunrays was breathtaking – a truly magical landscape, leading to an unknown reality.

I remembered my very first trip that had taken place two years earlier, for a study trip to Russia, when I was sixteen. Gazing out of the window, as the miles slipped away, my thoughts flew back to my first encounter with life abroad.

My university-level experience in Moscow was one of the reasons I had decided to pursue a university degree abroad. I fell in love instantly with the international atmosphere there. As much as I loved my life in Bulgaria, I had always aspired to experience something more than what I had been used to in my wonderful and comfortable world at home. I wanted to see and change the world, to thrive in a multicultural environment. I admired people, who were part of the Peace Corps, UN or Red Cross, traveling the world, making a change, helping others. I also aspired to use my skills on a broader and bigger scale, hence I'd always expected, eventually, to end up working, studying, training dancesport or travelling for a long period abroad. I had just never anticipated it was going to be so soon.

When I was a kid, no more than four or five years old, I had a favourite 'where to live' game, which we played with my cousin. We used to take our grandparents' dusty globe from the attic and spun it around. Then, on the count of three, we stopped it randomly by pressing our fingers onto its surface. We believed that someday we would either visit or live in all these unknown places around the world. I'd longed to experience something new, to travel, to explore and see the world, and I'd promised myself that I would make it happen when I 'grew up'.

My family was supportive of the fact that I was going to undertake my education in Denmark. However, it took me some time to convince them how much I wanted to go. I knew they loved me endlessly and that they wanted the best for me, but I also knew that my parents secretly hoped I would change my mind. For this reason, they insisted that I should have a 'broader' range of choice, and advised me to apply first for Sofia University (widely considered the best university in Bulgaria).

So I did. I remember sitting in the Sofia University auditorium during the preliminary history exam – a prerequisite for admission to the programmes I had applied for there – and wondering if it was meant for me to study there. The university was no doubt beautiful and the auditorium, despite crowded, seemed spacious and bright. My mind was racing, and I could not help but think how different my life would be if I had chosen to study in Sofia. It was not an easy choice, but it felt *easier*. While awaiting the announcement of the exam topic, I could somehow perfectly well picture what it would be like if I were to study in Sofia, at a distance of just under 400 km from my hometown – a six-hour bus ride, or twenty-five-minute flight. Even though I had not even started the exam yet, which was usually one of the toughest admission assignments in Bulgaria, the picture in my head felt safe, secure, predictable and comfortable. I knew that it represented the dream of many students. But it was not my dream. Even though I did well at the exam and was honored to receive an offer from one of the best universities in Bulgaria in my priority programme, my mind had already been made up a long time ago.

I firmly stood by my decision to pursue a higher education abroad, and to find a student job as soon as possible, in order to be independent and be able to support my studies. My choice did not feel safe or comfortable; quite the opposite, in fact. It felt uncertain and highly concerning. Excitement and anxiety took turns to overwhelm me. What if the study programme failed to meet my expectations? What if I could not manage to support myself financially? What if Jasen and I could not endure the long-distance?

But what if it turned out to be a once-in-a-lifetime, enriching experience beyond my imagination? There was only one way to find out.

I could never picture what my life would be like after I left home; I had no clue. Even before I had received my letter of admission to Aarhus University – or more accurately speaking, before I had checked the admission results online – I just knew that this was the road ahead for me. The physical letter of admission had come in my postbox several days after I already knew I'd been accepted. I remember, though, that when I found the actual letter with the university stamp and logo in the mailbox, I had gazed at it for a couple of long seconds, hardly blinking and being indecisive whether I should open it or not. What if it said something else? (luckily, it didn't).

This subconscious notion of what 'feels right', which no external forces can compare to, was my drive. This is the drive that pushes you to search for and fill in this 'something' that is missing. It is the force that calms the storms of the restlessness and replaces the feeling of uneasiness in your stomach; the feeling that you have to change direction, when you feel a permanent sense of dissatisfaction. I often perceived this as irrational. However, my main motivation for choosing Aarhus University in Denmark was not because it was the most logical and comfortable choice, but because it felt right. I just sensed that this was where I had to be.

There were several factors, which in their unpredictable ways, also supported my decision to consider studying abroad. Our lives are influenced by things that we often cannot control, all the time, and what matters the most is our response to them.

Of course, Aarhus University's top one hundred ranking in the world had a big impact on my choice. The reputation of the Danish quality of education and the fact that it was affordable for EU students were also highly significant factors. These were essential, and could be categorized as the 'main drivers' that I have always stated in interviews, when I have been asked the questions *'Why Denmark?'* and *'Why Aarhus University?'*

What I have never told people until now, was that the many years of professional dancesport[6] experience had motivated me to pursue my Business and Economics degree abroad. What do business and dancing have in common?

For more than ten years, dancesport was my biggest passion, and in my sixteen-year-old mind's beliefs, was my whole world. As a kid, I

---

[6] Competitive ballroom dancing, under the umbrella of the World DanceSport Federation, consisting of latin and standard dances.

was dancing all the time, and everywhere, so when I turned four, my parents thought it was a high time I stopped dancing with the furniture around the house, and signed me up for dance lessons. Starting as just a little girl's hobby, dancesport turned into almost a full-time outside of studying professional occupation.

I regarded this sport as the place where I felt safe, alive, invincible and extraordinary. Nothing could compare to that feeling of freedom I got when I was in a dance rehearsal or concert, performing at a competition, or on stage. It also turned out to be the one thing that broke my heart into a million pieces, when I had to say goodbye to the ballroom dancing. Before I stopped training professionally, I had always dreamed of continuing my dancesport development abroad. However, my life turned in a different direction, which I realized later was for the better. I had to find something else I believed in, something that was exciting me and was worth fighting for – and to conquer it. I was free to explore the new possibilities.

Saying goodbye to dancesport was a tough decision, but it opened the door to other new and amazing opportunities I had never considered.

There were many of them – and luckily, I found that dancing did not define me or my personality. Instead, it had installed certain traits in me during the years, such as drive, self-discipline, curiosity, determination and courage. These were the qualities that had formed my identity and character. The foundation was in place; the sixteen-year-old me needed to find a new passion – new goals and dreams.

Doing my university degree abroad was one of those new opportunities, and a big fraction of the inspiration came from the ambition and drive of a former dancer, who dreamed to train abroad. Ironically, studying business and management abroad was one of the new passions that, in turn, led to more exciting new goals, which filled the emptiness left by the sport. As it turned out, it was not time that was able to make me forget an old passion and move on, but it was a new, stronger one, which could ignite the flame and push me to keep moving forward.

My experience of the study trip to Moscow took place shortly after I had stopped training, and it kindled the ambition to challenge myself, broaden my horizons (experience, knowledge and networks), develop personally and professionally to the best extent possible and thrive in a multinational environment. I aspired having an international life, meeting and working with people from different backgrounds from mine. I'd always dreamed about travelling and experiencing new cultures and the study trip proved to me how much I wanted this.

After I came back from Russia, I started researching universities abroad. I remembered then that a friend of mine had talked once about business academic programmes taught in English in Scandinavia. Back then, I hadn't really listened.

After checking the universities in the Nordic countries, I'd put Denmark at the top of my higher-education list. The reason was simple. Aarhus University, Business and Social Sciences won me on first sight.

Besides the obvious ranking of this Danish university among the top in the world, as well as the fact that AU had my most preferred Bachelor's programme (Business Administration) taught in English, there was one last and decisive trigger. It may sound ridiculous, but it was a group of AU students I'd never met or talked to back then who helped me make up my mind and set my heart on Denmark and Aarhus University.

I saw them on the university website, standing as a group of students from the business school. One day, sitting in my room at home in Burgas, wondering which university to choose, my eyes crossed the face of one of them on the website – a confident looking student with blue eyes. I remember thinking, *'Dear angels and whoever else is listening from the Universe, I would like to make a wish. I would like to have the same confidence and the feeling of being in the right place as these students on the front page of the AU website'*. It was scary-fascinating how someone you have never met or talked to in your life could influence and inspire you so strongly. I had seen over a hundred advertisements of universities, but had never been influenced by anything else in such a way. Something about this picture of students seemed so sincere, that I was struck by it. And I could very well see and picture myself among this group of students. Every time I opened the AU website to check on something, I wished I knew them. I wished I was among them.

Choosing Aarhus University, Denmark as my number one priority was, as I recall, one of the best choices I have made so far in my life.

It may sound naive to you, and you may wonder, *'How could she let a photo influence such a big decision?'* I clearly remember the times I had been feeling insecure and concerned whether or how I would manage on my own in a foreign country. However, each time I saw the picture of the AU students I was reminded of where I wanted to be standing, and what I strived for. It gave me the assurance that I needed, without judging: only pointing out what I dreamed of. Quite a few times it saved me from giving up, and it managed to put me back on track with my initial goal.

***

Looking out at the already clear bright-blue sky, I was holding my breath for how it would be when we arrived in Denmark. Lost in thoughts and conversations with my travelling companions, I noticed that we had reached the Baltic sea, and were approaching the Danish coast. I remember seeing for the first time the Øresund Bridge[7] from above. The sight of it made me wish I could get the chance to travel across. Luckily, it did not take me long before I made that happen.

As the plane started its descent, I was counting the ferries, ships and boats that sailed through the calm sea, and it was then I saw one of the most powerful and breathtaking views I had ever encountered until that moment. Suddenly the dark blue water beneath us was full of offshore wind power turbines. I had never seen an offshore farm before, and I could not help but stare. It was a truly empowering sight, both literally and metaphorically.

The stunning sea-landscape, clustered with ships and wind turbines, slowly began to turn into a light-green, flat land. This beautiful transition of landscape was how Denmark stole my heart on first sight. Right there, I forgot all anxiety and concerns, everything just felt right.

Epilogue

I get goose-bumps each time I think about the circumstances and chain of events that had led one way or another to my decision to move to Denmark. I cannot believe how many little things could lead to this once-in-a-lifetime experience that changed my world

---

[7] The double-track railway bridge between Sweden and Denmark.

completely. No matter who or what triggers them, we are the only ones responsible for the choices we make. This aside, the best lesson I have learned from then was to trust my gut feeling and to rely on my own judgment. I have learned that you should choose the hard but exciting route, the one that does not seem 'safe' or 'clear', but makes you feel excited and alive. I learned that it is okay to fear what is ahead – following your dreams is not about being fearless, it is about having the courage and faith to keep trying. Take scary and big decisions on your own – as well as let them change your life.

If only I could whisper to the eighteen-year-old Misha back then, that in only four years, she would have an internship, student job and a Master's thesis cooperation for one of the biggest wind power manufacturing companies globally, followed by a career in one of the leading international shipping companies, I am sure she wouldn't have believed me.

Chapter Three – Reality-Check

How to Find Your Ground (During Your First Year Abroad)

I was sitting at my desk and drinking coffee from the recently received AU Alumni cup from the Aarhus University Master's graduation ceremony, which had taken place only a couple of days before. It was October 2014 – five years and two months had passed since I had arrived in Denmark for the first time. I could not believe that it was all behind me, that my higher education abroad had ended. Five unimaginable, amazing, but challenging years were over.

It was a rainy and windy day, and I wished the weather had stayed warm a bit longer. The summer before my Master's graduation had passed by too fast. Most of the period had been devoted to the finalization of my Master's thesis, which I did in a collaboration with a pioneering company in the renewable energy sector (wind power). The efforts were worth it, as I learned tremendously much from the project, and the final examination gave me the perfect finish of my higher education abroad with 12 (the top grade in Denmark). Aside of my final thesis, I had commitments towards my volunteer activities, along with my student job, travelling, and the preparation for starting my own company, which I launched soon after graduation.

It had been a busy but also very exciting and rewarding summer, and I could not have been more grateful. It had marked an end of an era: the end of my university journey in Denmark and the beginning of a new one. Looking down at my AU Alumni cup filled with what I call coffee but my Danish friends call 'milk with sugar', I felt a strong sense of accomplishment, which was only partly due to the newly acquired Master's degree. I knew well that the feeling of ease and relief was because I had made it all quite successfully on my own for five years in a foreign country. I was very young when the plane had taken off from Burgas Aiport to allow me to pursue my dream to study abroad, and despite all challenges and difficulties, I was ready for new adventures. If I could do that, I felt as if I could do anything.

Looking out of my apartment window, I thought of the day I'd arrived in Denmark and all the things that happened over the past five years – everything my family, friends and I had been through. The excitement and anticipation of building a new life from scratch, dealing with situations I'd never imagined possible, and thriving in an international environment. I got a flashback of the wonderful and crazy days and nights we had spent with my friends – studying, partying, cleaning up after the partying, developing ideas, travelling, talking about what the world held for us. We had been such a great support to each other that I could not imagine my life without the people I'd met in Denmark. Then, however, there was also the inevitable 'down' side of it all – being away from family for far too long, going through the long-distance relationship, the doubts and challenges that I had faced abroad. I had had to balance my time between student jobs, volunteer work and tough university schedules, covering the monthly fixed costs, and hardly being able to save for anything while being a student. It was difficult, but I would not give it up or exchange it for anything else – any of it.

Even though there were five years' difference between my 'grown up' twenty-three–year-old self, and the eighteen-year-old version of myself, the day that I had arrived in Kastrup Lufthavn[8] in Copenhagen for the first time felt like a lifetime ago.

While lost in memories and thoughts about whether I would manage to present the exact emotions of this day, I convinced myself to guide you not only through the day I arrived, but through the first weeks, as well, in order to illustrate and reflect upon the initial emotions and impressions of being an international student. I had no clue what the future there was going to hold for me, and I had this mixture of excitement and frustration hugged tight in my stomach.

***

---

[8] Copenhagen Airport in Kastrup.

August 2009

The train-trip with DSB[9] from Kastrup Airport, Copenhagen, to Aarhus Central Station gave me the possibility of observing and exploring Denmark's landscapes during sunset. The two sides of the railway were coloured with the little, cute Scandinavian houses – exactly like the cottages I had seen in my Hans Christian Andersen fairy tale book when I was a child. They resembled the Christmas chocolate gingerbread houses, only bigger and prettier. When we reached the bridge between Zealand[10] and Funen (Danish: Fyn), I felt I could stare forever at the endless view of the Baltic Sea, even though I had been living next to a sea my whole life. There were no mountains to be admired on the horizon, a sight I was used to when travelling in the beautiful countryside in Bulgaria, but everything was new, breathtaking and fascinating in its own way. The unfamiliar flat green landscape was in its own way magnificent, especially when I witnessed later how the sea merged with the valleys of Jutland (the peninsula starting the mainland of Denmark), accompanied by the occasional onshore wind turbines seen in the distance.

Perhaps because of the (still) warm weather, the endless fields of green grass, or the fact that I could not believe I was already travelling in

---

[9] The Danish National Railway Company.
[10] Sjælland in Danish, is the large island of Denmark, where the capital Copenhagen is located.

Denmark, I was wonderstruck. I was also extremely exhausted when we eventually reached Aarhus, and our destination for the day – the student housing, where a fellow AU student – Niya was kind to offer me a place to stay until I received the keys to my room.

When we reached the student estate, it was already dark, which was quite an achievement, considering that the sunset in Denmark during the summer was only after 23.30. That was how I knew we had arrived a bit past midnight, as I had lost track of time completely. After my travelling friends and I finally managed to get our luggage out of the bus and said 'good night', I followed Niya, my host, who met us at the bus stop, to where her student house was supposed to be.

'*Ah... what happened to the summer?*' I thought sadly, trembling in the cold evening and reflecting that I must have been more prepared. I remembered with nostalgia the warm summer nights in Bulgaria, where it had been so hot I could hardly breathe. *You should have got your jacket out of the luggage when you arrived in Denmark, you smart-ass,*' the annoying voice of rationality in my head reminded. It definitely didn't feel like home anymore, and as the sunset was gone, replaced by the cold Nordic wind, the magic was gone too.

While we were walking, I could hear a melody in the distance, getting louder as we approached the centre of the student housing, and my curiosity took precedence. I remember walking fast and trying to catch up when we reached a big square at the middle of the estate. The whole area was filled with hundreds of dancing and singing students. I felt jealous about how relaxed and easy-going they seemed, while I was cold, exhausted and fighting with all kinds of feelings: exhaustion from the trip, homesickness, anxiety about where I was going and what on earth had I been thinking leaving in the first place. Apparently, we had arrived at the middle of the annual summer festival. I noticed then the band standing up on the stage under the clear night sky, getting ready to start a new song.

'Alright, people!' the singer greeted the cheering crowd. *The next song is devoted to all new students and arrivals in Denmark! Welcome, guys! This is Bon Jovi, "It's my Life"!'* the lead singer shouted, and then gave a nod to the boys behind him, followed by a laud scream of approval from the crowd. How appropriate.

It felt as if the vibes of the familiar song took all the air out of the night. I forgot that I had to walk fast to follow Niya, and that I was tired and freezing; I just stopped and stood there, in the middle of the screaming crowd, with my luggage in my hands, and stared. The magic was back, and it was taking all the space around me. Right there, I felt in the right place. And this was how during my first hours in Denmark and Aarhus, I had managed (by accident) to attend – as I recall – a festival to remember.

***

Thanks to Niya, I was lucky to have a place to reside in Aarhus at the very beginning of my stay in the country, until I had received my own student-dormitory room offer very soon after that.[11] And thanks to her and my amazing new friends, I never felt alone during the first days. Most importantly, I managed to find successfully the university campus, all grocery stores nearby, the local post office, the train station, the bus stations and the nearest shops, where I could buy a local phone card. In other words, I could find all the basics and gradually climb Maslow's pyramid in a foreign context, which proved to be much more important than I'd thought when you land 'overseas' for the first time.

Prior to arrival in a foreign country, my experience has shown me that people (in that count also me) focus primarily on the bigger-scale planning. In my case, this included (not necessarily in this order): buying plane tickets, arranging the logistics about my new accommodation, sorting out the main concerns about the university application and admission, as well as the semester start, the introductory week activities, and familiarizing oneself with the course

---

[11] I strongly recommend all new international students applying for a student residence in Scandinavia to apply for the waiting lists of the student housing at least six months before their desired moving-in date, even if they do not know the admission results yet.

descriptions. All these were then followed by practicalities based around acquiring the necessary academic books, becoming familiar with the campus facilities, considering student job possibilities and career development opportunities, and being overtaken by the excitement of cooperating with people from all over the world, encountering new adventures, and doing some long-term planning.

Then, guess what? Post-arrival, and after the initial shock and jet lag are gone, you realize that all that matters is to find out where to buy water and food, how to connect to the Wi-Fi and where to buy a bus card and a local SIM card for your phone. These are often taken for granted, and are not given enough attention as part of the 'concern' list. However, all practical, basic needs are the foundation of everything else that follows once they are fulfilled.

Upon arriving at a foreign country, these are: finding out where to buy grocery (and what food you can find in the supermarkets), whether you can drink the local water from the tap, how to use the local transportation, how to stay connected with people (locally suitable adapter, internet accessibility, mobile card, and other), where to apply for the residence permit, and where you can find the laundry room. No matter how overwhelmed your brain is with 'greater things', without finding out the basics, you add unnecessary worries to the already stressful new and unfamiliar reality.

I was fortunate to be surrounded by people who could show me all the essential, practical things I had to know during my first days in the unknown surroundings. I strongly advise you to research the *where* and *how-to* in advance. Most universities send a newcomers' guides to the admitted international students, and in case you have not received such information, contact your university prior departure.

My first days in Denmark seemed unreal. I felt a mixture of fascination with my new world and astonishment that I was going to study at my top priority university. Yet I was overwhelmed by acquainting myself with the foreign environment, while feeling a great dose of nostalgia for home and my family, friends and Jasen. My head was spinning from looking around all the time, trying to absorb the architecture, the nature, the landmarks – I wanted to take in as much as I could from my new world. I felt like a five-year-old kid in Disneyland. I was also afraid that this was all a dream, that I would stumble and wake up any moment from. At the same time, I was feeling as if my heart had been ripped from my chest and left at home, in Bulgaria. I found myself in a place I had never been before, both geographically and metaphorically.

The first days of the Introduction Week at the Business Campus were indeed busy and entertaining, for which I was grateful as all the activities fully distracted me from feeling homesick. The programme was filled with information, new people, parties, many social and team-buildings activities, and yet more practical information. I felt this strong anxiety and excitement, which I am sure every new student also felt. I believe we did not get more than four hours of sleep per night during this first week.

I could not believe I was seeing all the surroundings 'live', and not on images. It felt exactly like visiting a famous spot or historic monument you have read about and seen on TV hundreds of times. Around me was the actual vision of everything that I had seen only in pictures before, while I was trying to imagine whether I could see myself 'fitting' there. This included the facilities of the university, such as our future study rooms, the business school's AULA (the large auditorium of the business faculty, with almost cathedral-like windows and fascinating wooden ornaments), the spacious library and bright corridors with their glass-to-ceiling windows, and the 'Klubben' (the university bar in the basement). Moreover, the city cathedrals, the cozy cafes and the picturesque Aarhus streets, the gardens and the Scandinavian architecture all around me were captivating beyond my imagination.

The business faculty, where most of my lectures were, seemed like a labyrinth to me – one that I could not wait to explore. The campus had so many buildings and auditoriums, with gardens and lakes in between, halls, bridges and facilities, which were stunning and confusing (even the senior students told us that they were still regularly getting lost). The school looked like a modern, magnificent Scandinavian castle.

However, I had always imagined myself in these places feeling happy, calm and relaxed. Even though everything looked a thousand times better live, I could not get rid of the enormous ball of anxiety that was stuck in my stomach. How could you be so happy and yet frustrated all at the same time? Apparently, it was possible during your first week in a new country, when you are an inexperienced eighteen-year-old.

No matter how friendly, kind and helpful the new people around me were, and how engaging and interactive the activities, festivals and meetings were during these first days, I could not help constantly feeling a huge emptiness. I was missing my family in Bulgaria painfully much. Every time I was left by myself, my thoughts did not leave me at peace. I did not even know whether I would have had the possibility to see Jasen for Christmas, with the first semester lectures calming down before the exam session in January. Even if I could have the chance to fly back, that would have been in more than five months – so it was likely that I wouldn't see him again for another six months, at least. The time that had to pass until then seemed endless.

The fact that we were extremely preoccupied by activities and information, followed by the new semester courses, lectures and tutorials, was a blessing, since I had little time to over-think and dwell on the mess of questions in my head.

However, everyone who knew that Jasen and I were having a long-distance relationship decided to tell me a *'I'm sorry to tell you this, but...'* story of a friend (of a friend), who had tried to do the same, and had not managed to sustain their relationship. Even though *'they really loved each other, you know...'*, as they trailed off.

Odds were clearly against us, and I was reminded constantly about it. The last months had felt like a honeymoon period. Everyone said that long-distance relationships were impossible – that they never worked. I was doing my best to keep the hope that Jasen and I were different, special, unique. We were crazy about each other; wouldn't that be enough? Wasn't love enough?

I had thought of the 'what if' scenario countless times: that one of us might meet and fall in love with somebody else during our two years' long-distance period. And I also thought about the odds of breaking up, because one of us could decide that we had had enough. After all, we were two teenagers in love, and a lot could happen during these twenty-four months – a lot had happened already, even during my first week in the new country. My environment was so dynamic that it seemed as if I had been away for one year, when it had only been a month. I missed Jasen all the time, no matter how much attention I was receiving, no matter how great, exciting and busy my life of a freshman abroad was, and I hated that he was not part of it. I wished he could be there with me. It was a story that everyone predicted the ending of. One, that I was determined to change.

When my first semester university classes started, I realized also that most of my classmates were either older than me, and thus more experienced, or that almost all of them already had some background in Business, Economics, Accounting, Statistics and our other subjects – fields of study that I was unfamiliar with. Everything that I knew or had done and achieved did not seem to matter anymore. It was a fresh new start, but I did not feel as if I had a head start, as I had thought. On the contrary, I felt behind. I also secretly envied my classmates from Denmark for having their families living close by, and thus for having the chance to visit them whenever they wanted.

Most of the students already had places to live, and were receiving monthly scholarships for attending university – something that you could not receive in Bulgaria, if you had chosen to study abroad. In contrast, what I had was a passion for international education and a pressing need to find a student job. You can be a star at home, but you are a stranger abroad, at least at the beginning.

In high school, I had developed the feeling that I did not need to prove anything anymore – I felt accomplished. On my own in a foreign country, I had to prove myself all over again – in a new, highly competitive and challenging setting.

One day in early September, during my second week in the country, I was sitting alone in the common room of Niya's place, holding tightly onto my coffee mug, as if it was going to make everything alright. It was raining heavily and the common room was quiet and empty, since it was not even 6.00 o'clock in the morning. Niya had sensed that something had been bothering me, and before I had realized, she had jumped onto the soft sofa, and was sitting next to me.

'How can I feel like I am in the right place, and yet the wrong place, all at once?' I asked Niya in despair. *'Did you ever feel like this, when you first arrived here?'* I turned to look at her.

What a sad and desperate picture I must have been at that moment!

'... You mean, during my first weeks in Aarhus, when all I wanted to do was to take my deposit back and get on the first plane back home?' Niya replied, smiling weakly.

'I have to admit that the thought has crossed my mind, as well,' I said, laughing at her honest reply, and encouraged by the fact that Niya was nevertheless still studying there and she was doing amazingly. I took a

deep breath and stopped whining. I was not exactly filled with joy right away, but there was a great feeling growing inside me: a determination to deal with the upcoming challenges, and to be open and patient for the opportunities ahead of me. No more moments of self-pity, I promised myself.

That was, I believe, my culture shock at its best (or perhaps its worse).

Culture shock is a stressful emotional state, resulting from trying to adjust to living in a foreign country, as well as to your new life as an expatriate. Not that my eighteen-year-old self knew anything about the concept. It wasn't until two years later, during the International Management class, when I could relate to and identify the culture shock as my own experience and as a norm for people moving abroad. Before that, I was just painfully aware that I had not been at peace with myself during the first months.

Not surprisingly, I found out later that many other international students felt the same way, which meant that this state of doubt and frustration had not been a unique experience for me alone. It was great that we, the international students, had each other as moral support, as we were going through the same. I remember my very first Christmas away from my family, during my first semester at Aarhus University; I could not fly back to Bulgaria due to the tight winter exams schedule, and because I wanted to save up some money by taking student working shifts during the holiday. Besides, even though I already had a student job in Aarhus, I'd decided that I did not have the extra money to buy an overpriced Christmas plane ticket.

I hated when the real Christmas trees died after the holiday, so I had made a small, paper tree, hoping Santa would forgive me. However, one of my classmates, who also had to stay in Aarhus for the holidays, sensing my (unhealthy) desire for a Christmas tree, brought his fir plant, to our Christmas Eve dinner. Yes, directly with the pot. The rest of my foreign friends covered it with decorations, so it eventually represented a real and remarkable Christmas tree. What I thought would be the most depressing Christmas in my life, turned into a wonderful night, and I had never cried out of laughter so hard. I am not going to bore you with Christmas tree stories, but my point is that your friends are your family when you live abroad – one of the most valuable lessons that I learned right away.

The bond you create with your friends abroad is irreplaceable

The first two times I had gone back home to Burgas to visit my family between the semesters, I had felt as if 'Denmark' had never happened, the moment I had stepped on home ground. Being back home felt like being in a parallel world, where everything was suddenly 'back to normal' and my experience in Aarhus seemed like something far away and unreal. It also seemed to me that little had changed in Bulgaria during that time, but everyone else had their own lives and for them things were progressing a lot, as well. Despite that my life in Denmark had been changing at such a fast pace, back in my childhood room in Burgas, I felt as if I had never left.

Then the same happened again when I went back to Aarhus. It always felt as if my week in Burgas with my family had been just a dream. Often I found myself wondering which 'life' was real. I hated the goodbyes that I had to make each time. It was a heartbreaking experience, every single time.

So, this is how it is going to be from now on? Hellos, followed by goodbyes? Each time I was saying goodbye, or as my Danish friends optimistically like to call it *'a see you later'*, I was trying to commit my parents' faces to memory. Because I knew that, as positive and true the claim of my friends was, our 'see you later' would be a minimum of another five months. This seemed like such a long time, and it was always hard to say, *'see you later'* after being around each other again. I developed a fear of 'getting used to'.

I also wondered whether this bewilderment would ever end. Each time I was going back and forth between the two countries, I was as confused and disoriented as I could be. I felt torn between my life in Bulgaria and my new world in Denmark, and I desperately wanted to keep pieces of both. My culture shock and reverse culture shock were fighting for taking turns, and I wasn't sure which one was strongest and deserved to win.

The first year abroad feels like clash of worlds

Eventually, with time, I got used to this 'clash of worlds', and I decided to change my perspective and feel lucky to have them – my home and family in Bulgaria, and my new home and life in Denmark, and to convince myself that they both were part of *my reality*. I decided to try to be at peace with myself. I say *'try'*, because I knew that it was going to take some time, but it was a start of something good, and my whole world in a moment had already changed forever. The frustration has gradually diminished, but I am aware now, years later, that it can never fully disappear. At least, I have learned how to tolerate it. I found out that all that was needed was time and a change of perspective.

The sudden and unexpected waves of nostalgia come rarely now and do not hit me as bad as they used to during my first year abroad. As busy as I was during my first weeks in Denmark, it rarely happened that I had a moment to be alone. However, each time I was by myself, nostalgia kept me company. It reminded me that it was going to be another several months until I would be able to see my family, Jasen and my old friends again. The thought of that made it hard for the eighteen-year-old me to breathe. These feelings seem too dramatic now, but I remember how I imagined and dreamed about them coming through the door, into the room, and sitting on the couch with me for a while; how great it would have been if they could.

I had read in many different magazines about integration in a foreign country: that, if you had gone to study abroad, you had to make up your mind about whether you wanted to live there in the long-run or not, as soon as possible. I disagree. Even though I could see their point – that you must prepare yourself and plan your future – I do not believe that you have to make up your mind about this decision from the start of your foreign education. As I illustrated above, even during my first week I had already changed my mind several times.

However, this did not mean that I did not study the local language, learn about the culture, travel the country, experience and learn new things all the time – quite the opposite. Despite not knowing what was about to happen next, I wanted to know and experience as much as possible about Denmark. If you are a soon-to-be new international student, my advice is to take your time, because your decision today will probably change several times in the next six months, or even tomorrow.

Give your new home a chance to win you over

Getting to Know a New World

What I advise every new expatriate to do is to not jump to conclusions, but to take their time to get to know a new country. After all, you cannot predict where the next opportunity will come from.

***

October 2014

It had taken time and effort for me, too, to make up my mind about what I wanted after graduation, but what had happened was that I had managed to make up my heart. I was thrilled about the idea of what it was going to be.

Even now, regardless of having a job that I love, living in my favorite city and being able to practise my passions too, I am still figuring out where I would like to be and what I would like to do – every day. With each passing day, new experiences, people, knowledge and situations influence us in one way or another, and inspire new ideas and career preferences. Change is always present, and I have learned that in a fast-paced international environment, it is inevitable.

Visualize the situation where suddenly you must leave the country you live in, if not for good, then for the next couple of years. You are forced to pack your bags and get on the plane right away. What would you feel? Sadness? Relief? Anticipation? Frustration? Excitement? This is the best test to find out how you feel about the city or country you are in. Give yourself time to experience, and do not feel forced to make this choice during the first months in the new country. If my younger self had imagined that I had to pack my bags because I was forced to leave the country during my first weeks in Denmark, one of the overwhelming feelings would have been probably a *relief*. If I am forced to imagine that now, however, the feeling would be a despair.

These feelings are extremely individual, of course. Many of my (international, but also Danish) friends left the country after the completion of their studies. Most of my international friends live in their home countries now, but a few have moved somewhere else abroad. Some of my Danish friends, who had experienced living abroad for longer than a year, have also pursued an international career or education outside of Denmark afterwards. Fortunately, there are many roads and options to choose from, and I have learned that choosing the less predictable and less comfortable road makes dreams come true.

Epilogue

I absolutely believe that home is where your family is, the place where you grew up, where you dreamed about what the world and future might hold.

After embracing my world as a global citizen, I however also strongly believe that home is where you feel at the right place. Therefore, instead of feeling like someone with no real home, I feel extremely happy and lucky to be a person with two places called home in the world. Happiness is about how you perceive the world – regardless of where you are. I learned that it is a choice.

During my first year abroad, my environment was very dynamic, and I was always surrounded by many people, new friends, as well as wonderful classmates and colleagues. Yet I had never felt so lonely in my life. My cultural identity was a mess. The confusion brought of life-shifts, and a fast-paced, constantly changing environment, accompanied by culture shocks, did not last 'forever' as I had initially feared, but it took me more than one year to adapt to my multinational life as an international student. The transition takes time and energy, and requires patience. It is challenging and demanding, even exhausting, but also exciting and intriguing, all at once. Accepting your new reality as a global citizen is a process that inevitably involves a clash of worlds, even when the cultures are 'relatively' similar. I learned that, in practice, there is no such thing as 'relatively' similar cultures. You should be prepared that there will be always new, unfamiliar circumstances, and different customs, values and perspectives.

An important lesson I would like to share with you is that the friends you make abroad are in most cases your friends for life. They become your family and your anchor abroad.

What I also learned was that the 'distance' itself had nothing to do with whether a relationship survives or not. It is nonetheless a comfortable excuse for giving up a relationship, which has not worked out for other reasons.

You either love each other and want to be together, and therefore work for that, compromise, love, try hard, go to sleep, wake up and do it all over again, but eventually make it through, or you do not – regardless of any physical distance. If there is something already missing in the relationship, then it is not the distance but the circumstances (developing and growing in different surroundings, meeting new people, getting emotionally separated, among others) that increase the gap between two people. I cannot imagine letting the love of your life slip away because you are some (thousand) miles apart. The psychological reaction to the 'distance' is also what can make a significant difference in the development of the relationship. Make up your mind that with effort, the distance would not matter, and it won't. I learned that it all comes down to (at the risk of sounding like a popular love song) whether you really, truly desire to be together.

Long-distance relationships are not impossible; they are relationships with a specific obstacle. 'Difficult' is definitely not the same as 'not possible'; it is rather a test. Sometimes this test comes way too early in the relationship, as it did with Jasen and me.

Moreover, I learned that nothing should be taken as granted, and in order to get what I want from life – from my education abroad, career and personal life – I had to be in charge of my own fate. This can be hard to believe when you are eighteen years old. However, now I do not expect somebody else to get me 'out of the corner' and I know that courage, drive and determination must always come from me.

Even before I moved abroad, I had found out that I always had to fight for the things that I wanted in life – and make them happen. The most amazing things that have happened in my life have been the result of my own courage to come out into the spotlight – not because somebody else has picked me up and dragged me centre-stage. However, you need the support of your family and friends, to make great things!

Follow your passions, big ideas and dreams, with courage and drive, and be the best person that you can be. The rest, I learned, falls into place.

How to Thrive Abroad

Looking ahead – to the future. October 2014, Illustration by C'MNKY Art

Chapter Four – Breaking the Room of Glass

From Surviving to Thriving

Many studies have been written about expatriates' adaptation in foreign settings, due to the vastly increasing globalization and one of its many consequences: the growing number of students and professionals who live 'cross-cultural' lives. What made an impression on me was that scholars widely discussed the phenomenon called the 'Expatriate U-curve of Adjustment', which comprises the emotional states that the newcomers experience abroad.

The U-curve is a hypothesis – a process starting with a short period of initial astonishment and is then followed by culture shock, which leads to the phase of acculturation, and lastly ends with the adjustment of the expatriate to the foreign culture. When we studied the Expatriate Adjustment at university, I always tried to relate to the phases of the 'curve' listed by the books and journals. Everything seemed logical to me, but also incomplete. Reality is much more complicated, and people experience living abroad very differently. I found out that you could not put a timeline on integration.

Culture shock has mostly been described as the worst and 'darkest' phase. However, I do not think the culture shock, as explained in books and academic journals, is the worst you can encounter as a newcomer abroad. I had experienced my '*I am living so far away from my family!*' shock, and my 'international identity' confusion due to the shifts between cultural and social environments. I would imagine these are rather unavoidable. Yet what I experienced later was much stronger than culture and identity shock.

***

February 2011

Approximately one and a half years after I had arrived in Denmark, which was during my second year of my Bachelor's degree, it seemed as if I had it all figured out abroad. I already felt somewhat integrated culturally, and was surrounded by many good new friends. My family was healthy, happy and doing well. Back then, Jasen and I had already managed successfully through most of the long-distance period and it was going great. Jasen had done his best to visit me in Denmark as many times as possible, and I had been doing my part by travelling to Bulgaria at least every winter and summer, after the final exams were over.

I loved my life in Aarhus, too. The university and the education with its diversity, social activities, interactive sessions and all it was offering us thrilled me. The campus itself was fascinating – just like I had always imagined, if not better. My instincts had been right. This was confirmed each time I entered the university building – I felt that I must be in the right place.

The green gardens, the lakes with ducks at the very middle of the university, not to mention the beautiful surroundings and Nordic architecture with the typical Danish brick buildings, made me wonderstruck. The campus itself was a stunning combination of heritage and modernization. I also liked that the education in Aarhus University represented a teaching model, where we worked with real-life business practical cases. Most of the exams were 'open-book' format, which meant that the students could use all materials such as books, articles and internet during the exam. This was so since we were asked to reflect on theories, to solve the challenges, and apply the results of journal papers and book materials, instead of purely learn them by heart and 'repeat' theoretical models. The study environment was organized in such a way that collaboration and group work was widely encouraged, besides the individual assignments.

I had already spent enough time in the country to build some very strong friendships – I had friends from all over the world, we supported each other a lot and had a great time together. I believed I was doing very well academically too.

I also had a nice place to live in Risskov (my favourite area in Aarhus, together with the park of Aarhus University and Marselisborg strand)

and had a student job to support myself financially. I was having a good time outside of studying and work, had interesting courses, was studying Danish, and every time I walked around Aarhus's beautiful, hyggeligt[12] streets or entered the university campus, I felt as if I were living a dream.

Seems like the perfect life of a young, international student? Probably yes, except that I did not feel fulfilled, nor happy. I was constantly sensing this big, hopeless emptiness inside me, which this time had nothing to do with the fact that my family and boyfriend were living miles away. I could tell that something was missing, but I could not figure out what it was, and it was torturing me. I was mad at myself for feeling miserable, when it seemed as if I had it all. For the first time in my life, I was not feeling like myself. Things were just as I had always dreamed of and had imagined, but somehow everything seemed meaningless. I remember that I was helpless, trying to identify what was happening to that restless, self-motivated and ever-desiring-to-change-the-world girl, with a burning passion for life? The girl that always found happiness even in the most ordinary, grey days? The sense of unease in my chest was unreasonable and unexplainable.

---

[12] The word is used by Danes to express a feeling of enjoying life and being cozy. See Chapter 5 for a further explanation.

It felt as if I was locked in a room of glass. This is what I call being trapped in a psychological state that I choose to describe as a 'survival' mode. I cared about passing my exams, securing the student housing rent for the coming month, saving up for my ticket back to Bulgaria to visit my family, and I had allowed my mind and time to be almost fully occupied with these concerns and practicalities. I was lacking the drive that had always led me through in life, but the worst thing was that I did not know what to do to have it back. I cannot count the times when I caught myself thinking of packing and leaving the country before or after graduating with my Bachelor's degree. I desperately needed a change – and it felt that a change of place was the only way out.

Then each time this thought crossed my mind, a panic wave followed. Before these emotions could take over, I remembered how hard I had worked for this dream to come true. Consequently, I gave up the idea of leaving, and tried again to deal with the frustration. The circle was repeating itself. I had never felt such desperation and confusion in my life before. I had always been the persistent one, the one with the solution, the clear vision and the well-structured plan, and somehow it had always worked out well, until then.

I was absolutely 'on top of things', yet emotionally reaching the bottom. I never knew the combination was even possible. Was I depressed? Was I being unthankful? Did I demand too much out of life? Was I bored? I was feeling trapped, in what seemed to be a circular glass room with no windows, or exits. I could see the world outside, moving, spinning, progressing, but it felt to me as if I was not a part of it.

I know this sounds like a cliché, but the Universe – at least I hope and I believe – has its ways to pull us back from the edge, just when we are about to fall off the cliff into deep waters, and this was the case with me too.

One school day just like any other at Aarhus School of Business, at the beginning of my fourth semester, I was nearly late for the first tutorial of a new mandatory class. When I entered the tutorial room, I noticed a tall man standing in front of the class, not that much older than me, who was patiently waiting for everyone to find their seats. He said that his name was Sebastian,[13] and that he was from Denmark, currently a Master's student on campus, and that he was going to be our tutor for this class. He seemed very familiar, but I could not recall meeting him elsewhere. Before he started the tutorial, he made a short introduction about himself and the activities he was engaged in. Listening to this, I thought, '*He is extremely proactive, motivated and driven… he must really like what he is doing and knows where he wants to go… reminds me of myself when I*

---

[13] The name is changed for protection of privacy.

was in Bulgaria'. This thought scared me, as it reminded me of who I *was*, before I was burdened by the concerns of how to survive in a foreign country.

This was the wake-up call that helped me find a way to break the routine. I had not come to Denmark to survive; I was there to explore, grow, learn and succeed.

The more days passed of the new semester, the more inspired I was by this student – our new tutor, whom I hardly knew, but who reminded me so much of the person I had been in my home country. I had researched the organizations and initiatives Sebastian had mentioned in the first class, and I loved most of them. '*How could I never have considered these, during the past one year I have been in Denmark?*', I thought, quite disappointed. I'd never known about some of them, to start with, because I had let myself go 'head over heels' into my concerns over practicalities, learning Danish, having enough money to pay for rent and travelling, passing the exams, and living for the moment when I could see my family again. I needed to feel safe and sound, which was why, I realized, I had created a zone of comfort. My glass-room bubble. You know there is a lot more out there, you can see it, but you do not dare to escape, nor you know how to. And I was tired of it. During my second year abroad, after all the initial excitement and novelties of the first months were over, I had forgotten to actually long for my dreams and professional development.

Every time Sebastian and I talked, I was feeling like my inner compass was getting fixed – and that was exactly what I needed. It was also ironic how he believed more in me, than I did myself.

What I realized was that I had lost track of my real goals and my vision and sense of purpose, and was lacking the inspiration and drive that used to kick me into being better and aspiring for more.

I started allocating time for joining all the events and organizations I considered useful and relevant, which gave me back the passion for setting new goals and curiosity to explore, which I always used to have. The experience introduced me to new and interesting people, helped me find and engage in causes I cared about. I started participating in business case competitions, joining student unions, and I also plucked up the courage to apply for study-relevant student jobs, instead of my comfortable job, which was ensuring the monthly rent. I gained new competencies and discovered which business areas I was good at and aspired to develop.

I found that being highly proactive had simply not been enough for me. I was lacking the *passion* for doing things and the *vision* of where I was going. Thanks to meeting someone like Sebastian, I was back on my path to self-actualization, back to the motivated person I had always been before 'the room of glass'. I had a purpose.

Finally I could see new ways of learning, exploring and improving that I had never thought possible and I was able to set more precise goals. This was how I found my new 'love' in the face of Entrepreneurship, and Business Development and Strategy. This led to graduating with honors my Master of Science degree from Aarhus University, and starting a career soon after.

Looking up to someone, who was also taking the same road (not the expatriate one, but the road of the business-school student), witnessing his confidence, motivation and determination, I also gained the confidence to start looking for a better study-relevant student job right away. Namely, a student job, which would not be just enough for me to 'survive' in the foreign country, but one, which would give me valuable knowledge of *my core competencies and what I was most enthusiastic about.*

It took me time, persistence and a lot of effort, but the journey helped me develop – not to mention that I improved tremendously academically, and I did manage to get such a fantastic study-relevant job, eventually. Moreover, as I believe, it was one of the reasons, two years later, that I received my top internship offer from a big international company in Denmark, in my field of interest.

Thanks to meeting a role model like Sebastian, my perspective had changed significantly, and all seemed like a completely new world to me. It was intriguing, inspiring and energizing. It was not a 'dead-end' anymore. Most importantly, for the first time since I had arrived abroad, I was starting to feel like home in Denmark. I even started missing Aarhus insanely when I was travelling abroad.

The glass around me was broken; I was set out free.

Gone! The never-resting thought of packing and leaving was long gone. Giving up and running away…? Not today.

Sometimes I catch myself wondering what would have been if I had never met Sebastian that year and I am grateful I did not have to ever find out.

Therefore, I do not believe that culture shock is the worst you can experience during your expatriate life. What I do believe and did experience, though, was that it was extremely easy and dangerous to 'lose track' of who you want to be, while focusing on 'surviving' in a foreign country.

What is the main lesson out of the experience I just shared with you?

Having a vision and incorporating your values into your career and academic life is what will kindle the light of progress. Stephen Covey

(1989) illustrates repeatedly the importance of genuine purpose, inspiration and goals in his book *The 7 Habits of Highly Effective People*, recommended to me some time ago by a good friend of mine – and I strongly recommend it to you for more reading on the subject.

I believe I have been self-motivated in 99% of my life. Nevertheless, when living in a foreign country, the remaining 1% may trap you in the suppressing room of glass. Inspiration and vision are the key drivers, which will help you break free from the survival mode. Once you do, aspire to help and make a difference for someone else, as well. He or she may need you more than you know.

***

November 2011

I remember it was a sunny, warm November day – a lovely surprise for a Danish autumn. I was in my fifth semester of my Bachelor's degree, and I was sitting in the AU library, with the most recent edition of the student magazine from Studenterlauget, one of the biggest student unions in Denmark. I often read the newspaper for the sake of mastering my Danish language reading skills (and because I secretly enjoyed all campus-related articles). I was such a geek sometimes.

Skimming through the magazine, while at the same time trying to find the academic chapters I had to read for my Economics course, I stumbled upon a short interview with Sebastian. It was regarding his (back then) internship. There was a small picture of him attached to the interview. He was smiling, looking so happy, and I could not help smiling back.

'*Oh, wait a second…*' I suddenly remembered something. I spoke aloud, ignoring the confused looks of the fellow students around me.

Looking at his picture in the magazine, I finally realized where I knew him from. Sebastian had been one of the students from the AU poster and website, who had originally inspired me to make up my mind to apply for Aarhus School of Business. On top of this, one year later, he had played a huge part in how I found a reason and purpose to stay.

'*As it turned out, you helped me twice, in fact, without even knowing it,*' I thought, smiling at the irony – what an interesting coincidence. The Universe had a good sense of humor.

Somewhere, some time ago, I read that the people in our life do not have to always deliberately do something to have an impact on us – they simply need to be.

PS: Shortly after I had completed my Bachelor's degree in 2012 and was about to start my Master's at Aarhus University, I had been invited to participate in the Aarhus University Catalogue, and later for the new Website Campaign 2013/2014, as the spokes-student of the BSc(b) –

Business Administration study line. Interesting how things turn out, I thought when I said 'yes' to the offer. During my studies, I was also a student ambassador of Aarhus University, Business and Social Sciences for the new international students, have been a guest speaker at career events, and had done interviews and testimonials aimed at helping the foreign students find their ground abroad. I have been up to anything that could be of value or help to other international students integrate and make the right choices, because I believe that the sharing of knowledge and inspiration is the best support in the world. I found that firsthand.

Epilogue

The 'glass room' is a comfort zone bubble. I believe that this occurs after the overcoming of the culture shock and can be summarized as 'trapped in routine and survival' mode, due to lack of vision and purpose, replaced by everyday concerns.

My experience shows that the best way out is to find a mentor – someone who inspires, encourages and motivates you, and most likely has a career in your field of interest (but not necessarily). Then, be proactive, and ask for advice. Allow yourself to be inspired by someone whom you sincerely admire. Pay attention to their actions – how are they achieving their goals? Look at what education, volunteer work, network forums and career decisions have taken them where they are. You do not have to replicate their steps, but if you find something useful and beneficial – use it as an example and go your own way (see Chapter 6).

In Bulgaria, I was always aspiring to be a champion in everything that I decided to put my heart and head into. I thought that I would be the same highly driven person in Denmark from the start, too, but my first year abroad faced me with more challenges than I had anticipated. As it turned out, all I needed was a change of perspective, thanks to having a mentor and building a vision again.

Lastly, be open to offer help and advice to people – you will be surprised to find out what a great source of inspiration and a role model you can be for someone else, without realizing it, as Sebastian was for me.

Chapter Five – The Local Habits

What Does Acculturation Look Like?

When I moved to Denmark in 2009, I craved various Bulgarian foods, clothing brands, drinks and confectionary goods that I had grown up with. During the first months (and my first year) of living in Denmark I was surprised and disappointed to find out my favourite products simply did not exist there. Every time I travelled back to Burgas, I was on a mission to buy as many of the 'things' I had been missing back in Denmark as possible. I could not imagine coping another way.

Six years later, without even realizing it, my taste and preferences had changed tremendously. There are some things, however, that nothing can substitute – I never miss out on having the traditional Bulgarian cheese-cake 'banitsa' from the local bakery (and at home, made by mum or my grandmums – the one I prepare never gets that good!), but many other 'special treats' such as chocolates, pastries and beverages, have found their match in Denmark. My taste now, as with everything else, is a mixture of Danish and Bulgarian local favourites.

This chapter covers the adjustment and integration stage of (intentionally or not) adopting local cultural customs, language, habits and traditions, which are no longer perceived as 'foreign' and 'strange'. Scholars describe it as the main second-culture learning. People reach this point of integration at their own pace, regardless of whether they intend to stay for a long period in their new 'home' country or not. I believe that it is also the point where you stop perceiving yourself as a foreigner or expatriate, and when you start regarding yourself as a global citizen with a mixed identity. It is not about substituting your home-culture favorites, but instead building upon that and enriching it by the new experiences.

In order to illustrate best what this could be, I have prepared the list with some of the *Danishness* that I have adopted subconsciously during the past years.

Having playlists full of Danish songs

Not just for the sake of learning Danish, or not entirely at least, but mostly because I keep wishing I could do the accent. This will probably never happen, I found myself thinking, while my playlist featured Mads Langer singing 'København'.

Speaking of music..

Attending numerous festivals

Concerts by local Danish artists, international singers and bands, the jazz festivals, the culture nights – they are everywhere, all year round!

Danes know how to make a great party and open-air concerts to remember!

Aarhus Festuge (Aarhus Festival), for example, offers each year a wide range of new and established artists, diverse performances and concerts all over the city. Copenhagen Annual Jazz festival in July, on the other hand, lasting for almost two weeks, brings an irresistible holiday atmosphere to the city 24/7. There is also the opportunity to attend the wild Northside Festival and the Roskilde Festivals, which are arranged each year.

I have had the absolute pleasure of participating in an Apples Festival at the spectacularly beautiful city called Ebeltoft together with some of my best friends in Denmark. The city offered the best apple-treats you can imagine, food markets, games and chill-out country music.

More than that, thanks to the Silkeborg Festival, I had the delight to be at a concert of Mads Langer (one of my favourite Danish singers) and to hear 'Elephant' live. It was simply amazing! I have also been to the concerts of many other famous Danish artists that I like, such as Marie Key, Lukas Graham, Camille Jones, which have also left a mark. Not that all the fantastic concerts and the many visiting artists stops my Danish friends (or me) from travelling to concerts abroad. I realized I have developed a new strong passion for festivals and concerts.

Costume parades, marathons, the annual Distortion street party taking over the whole of inner Copenhagen, Sculptures by the Sea bi-annual festivals, Tivoli concerts, and so many more events form the spectacular, open-minded festival cultures of the Danes. And I still cannot get enough of it.

Running

As you might have already assumed, a lifestyle with a lot of festivals and drinking is the Danish lifestyle. However, a healthy lifestyle with many sports activities, biking and running is the other fundamental part. I had always been doing a lot of jogging, even during the 'Pre-Denmark' period of my life, so this wasn't exactly a newly discovered and adapted activity. However, my 'Post-Denmark' version is upgraded with the 'right' training clothes and equipment for outdoors cardio training – suitable for workouts in rain, wind and snow. Speaking of the last element, I am proud to say I have been also doing open-air training classes in wintertime with my colleagues, thus overcoming my fear of doing fitness outdoors in -10 degrees Celsius, in the dark, and last, but not least – in pouring rain.

Enjoying amusement parks

Denmark turned out to be the home country of the world's oldest amusement park in the world – Bakken. It is a fantastic place for the whole family, and is only ten minutes away by train from Copenhagen.

I cannot believe it took me four years before I visited Tivoli for the first time. Tivoli Haven is the world's second oldest amusement park – again with Danish roots. It is a magical place that I cannot get enough of! Meanwhile, it took me five years to pay a visit to Legoland – another amusement park located in a city called Billund. Legoland is a must-see, especially if you had been a LEGO fan as a child. When I was a kid (well, understand, until the point I graduated high school) I never knew that my favourite LEGO was a Danish brand. I only discovered this post-arrival in Denmark. After that I expected to find out that Santa Claus is also a Dane.

Wearing costumes at parties

During my time at university, our gatherings were accompanied by too many litres of øl[14] and, of course, by the dear old *danske* snaps – the Danish drinking heritage 'from the Vikings' (or so I was told). Nothing new, you might think. What left me wonderstruck, however, was how

---

[14] Danish beer.

everyone was wearing costumes at parties (and I do not mean just at Halloween, Fastelavn[15] and Christmas or New Year's Eve). And the down-to-earth, easy-going locals find this extremely normal.

Let me tell you, when Danes go to a costume party, they go all in. I remember the first time I had to attend a themed event. I showed up in a black dress and wearing a domino mask, out of fear of being overdressed. I had never thought that I would feel like the strange one among a group of 'vampires, witches and zombies'.

Already during the Introduction Week at Aarhus University, all Bachelor programmes were divided into different teams, each dressed in its own theme for a Botanical Garden party. My group was dressed under the 'Adams family theme' – gothic, vampire-like costumes, whilst there was a 'Harry Potter' group, 'The Mask of Zorro' team, a class with a Mexican theme and many more. You can imagine what a 'spectacular' sight we must have been. As it turned out, this was just the beginning of a costume-party series.

Riding a bike in the freezing winter as a daily transportation

… in snow, in wind, in (what it feels like) -50 degrees. However, I must admit that I am personally not a big fan of cycling to work in extreme

---

[15] Traditional Scandinavian carnival, celebrated in February.

weather conditions (especially in freezing temperatures), but my boyfriend rides his bicycle when everything outside has frozen – despite my mumbling. So let us say this is my favourite Danish habit as an expatriate, but this expatriate is not me.

Loving gulerodskage – the Danish cake with carrots

In Bulgaria, we have jokes about the cake with carrots and its flavour. To my surprise, ironically, it was one of the most popular cakes in Denmark. And the joke was on me, as it turned out to be delightful. The lesson: never make fun of anything you have not tried before.

Not suppressing my sarcasm

I have finally found a place where people are not offended by my (sometimes) sharp, direct and sarcastic remarks, even when they are obviously innocent and clearly ironic.

Answering 'ja' with an inhalation

It has taken me five years to notice that my *Viking* friends often express agreement by breathing the air in, instead of by breathing out. However, I am no longer questioning how such comes out naturally, as according to the people close to me, I do it rather often as well, apparently even when I speak Bulgarian.

Buying Christmas decorations in October

Jasen and I spent two hours of our Sunday afternoon in early October doing grocery shopping in one of the biggest retailers in Denmark. Shopping of any kind is not on top of my favourite free-time occupation activities, which made this an achievement. The reason was that I had spent half (or all?) of this time at the Christmas toys shelves, choosing a Christmas chocolate calendar. I know I was not supposed to have one before December, and especially considering it was still *October*, but was it fair to have the gorgeous decorations and Christmas treats already out, before Halloween was even over? In Bulgaria, I could hardly remember seeing any decorations before my birthday in mid-November. Ah, and the cafes – all of them playing their Christmas playlists in mid-October. Not that I complain at all, though. It gives people the Christmas spirit already in early fall, and from a marketing perspective makes us all spend more than we intend on Christmas decoration (candles, toys, sweets, *chocolate calendars*). It also gives me a motivation for doing grocery shopping after work.

Becoming a goodwill ambassador for equality

When I came to Denmark to pursue my higher education, I had read about *'Denmark: the classless society'*, which I thought was perhaps exaggerated. However, my experience showed that the statement is not that far from the reality. The Gini coefficient in Denmark, which is an index showing how big the gap between the income's division is, is one of the smallest in the world, according to the United Nations (UN) and the OECD[16] Income Distribution Database (IDD). Simply explained, when it comes to income, this means that the distribution is relatively equal, due to the country's welfare system. The minimum wage per hour in Denmark (as per 2016) is approximately 14 USD – one of the highest in the world, which partly explains why the gap is respectively one of the smallest in the world. The Danish welfare system is also characterized by free education, healthcare and childcare. Expectedly, the equality-based system is grounded on higher taxes, which can reach up to around 60 % of the income. No doubt, the Danish (or also referred to as the Scandinavian) welfare model, where all citizens have rights for social security, is ensuring economic growth and is admired.

Falling for Nordic design

I fell in love with the Scandinavian architecture from first sight – from the fairy-tale-like houses and the colourful buildings, to the exquisite stores and cafes, and I have admired it ever since I arrived in Denmark. What I like the most is the minimalistic Scandinavian interior. Danish

---

[16] The Organization for Economic Cooperation and Development.

designer Poul Henningsen's classic lamps, which I had initially noticed all over Aarhus University, are one of my favourite local designer items, together with the brand Royal Copenhagen and the stylish Danish jewellery bracelets and charms.

Enjoying the Nordic cuisine

The following list expresses my taste, which constantly changes, so I need to point out there are plenty more awesome drinks and treats that Denmark and its bakeries can offer.

- Rugbrød – Danish rye bread with seeds, which is a staple in the Danish food culture. If, in the past, preferring rugbrød over the 'white' bread was a rare thing for me, now buying any other type of bread is. In Bulgaria, the rye bread is not popular (partly because the local bread is also delicious), and the only people buying it from the retailers are the foreigners. Well, guess who is a foreigner also.

- Kanelsnegler (Danish cinnamon rolls) – when I was ten years old, I had an encyclopedia about the traditions of the different countries around the globe. I remember these cinnamon cakes illustrated under Scandinavia, where Denmark was presented, and I wished I could one day have the chance to try them. The grown up me found out they are much more delicious than they look, and were worth waiting for.

- Smørrebrød – clearly, I am a bread and cakes lover... This dish is famous in Denmark as the open sandwich. Despite what Danes say about the right combination of *frikadeller* (known to the world as meatballs), vegetables and herring or fish in general, my Danish friends eat this bread with pretty much everything on top. I like it in combination with butter, salad, salmon, eggs and shrimps. It was this beverage during my first days in Denmark that made me fall in love with Danish cuisine.

- Iced chocolate milk – if I tried to order such in a café elsewhere, I would be asked, *'Excuse me, didn't you mean a hot chocolate?'*

- Søde suppe (sweet soup with fruit) – the first time I tried the spicy soup with fruits (apples, pineapples and orange) at my company's canteen, I thought that there must have been a mistake, or that the soup had been prepared as a 'special edition' for visiting partners from abroad. As it turned out, I had not been introduced to the fact that the søde suppe was part of the New Nordic Cuisine.

Despite all, I still have a (non-)surprisingly low tolerance to lakrids (in Danish, i.e. liquorice or licorice in English) and everything that may contain it or smell of it. I had thought that after some time, I would have immunity against it. That has not happened yet. Danes are liquorice lovers. If you have never been in Denmark, you will be surprised to find out how many goods (and sweets) contain liquorice. Then, you can also try the salted liquorice, which is extremely popular in Scandinavia, if you are up for experimenting (but don't say I didn't warn you).

I had been tricked countless times by innocent-looking ice creams, chewing gum (*'What is wrong with this chewing gum?'* I asked my friends once, because I was convinced that it had expired), all mixed packages of candies, drinks, pasta, cakes, and the list goes on. I learned to be extremely wary of all chocolate resembling 'sweets' in Denmark. I remember the first time in my life I stumbled upon what unexpectedly turned out to be a liquorice candy. I was attending an event with the Finance and Consulting Club Aarhus organization at my university campus. I spat out the (what appeared to be a delicious, chocolate) candy very inelegantly into my hands, right after tasting it, in front of dozens of students, partner companies' representatives and consultants. Classy.

However, now I must make an exception to the above by admitting that the liquorice tea that a Danish friend of mine *forced* me to try was miraculously good. My family, who are crazy about that strange Danish treat (apparently, I am being the 'weird' one in the family), adored it too. Therefore, like it or not, I bring liquorice treats with me each time I fly back to Bulgaria, and I feel like such a cheater.

Tolerating insects

I admire how my Danish friends always give insects a chance to escape outside, and do not fear them coming into the apartments. Or do not care. In Bulgaria, everyone has an 'anti-insect safety net' on their windows, even though there are no dangerous bugs there either, and I have hardly seen a home with one in Denmark.

In contrast, let me illustrate a scene in my apartment when a huge bug was found creeping around:

'There's a bug on the curtains!' a friend of mine screamed during our otherwise relaxing coffee time. My first reaction was: *'Tell me it's not green!'* (I hate green insects). She assured me that it looked brown to her. *'Quick, get me something heavy!'* she requested. I grabbed the closest thing that looked heavy, which happened to be the Strategic Management book (desperate times, desperate measures) and handed

it proudly to my friend. '*Oh no, what is this? Not that heavy...*' she protested. '*Where is the "Basic Economics"?*'

Do not get me wrong, I always let bugs escape, but sometimes when a huge, multi-legged spider (or a green insect) invades the house, it is hard for me to turn on the Danish '*just wait for it to go out of the window*' attitude.

Appreciating the sunny days

I have always been longing for sunny and bright, warm days, and to live in a place made of only floor-to-ceiling windows, if that was possible, so I could get the most of the sun when it is up. However, I learned how to appreciate the sunlight once I moved to Denmark. Sometimes, during winter, we hardly see it for weeks. I also admire how Danes are always out, barefoot on the grass, or lying down without blankets, as long as there are sunny days. People exploit the good weather as much as they can, even if it means having a severe sunburn for a week.

Watching for cyclists when getting off the bus

Always and everywhere. Getting off a bus in Denmark involves careful evaluation of the cycling path, which is situated right between the station and where the bus stops. Before you cross it, you must watch out first for the passing bikes (which are usually like an invasion) before going on. I think this habit is something only people who have lived in Denmark can understand.

Craving for all these gardens and green areas

Wild animals, wandering deer, and forests at the very heart of the city?! Ja, tak! This is not something unusual for a Danish city, and I appreciate how all wild creatures are left in peace, and how people enjoy their free time lying on the grass or playing sports in the parks, when the weather is (considered) good. That is anything above 12 degrees Celsius, accompanied by sunshine.

When Jasen and I moved in together into our small but cozy student apartment in Aarhus we were pleasantly surprised to find out there was also a little green backyard. As it turned out, this yard was regularly visited by little, cute, and sometimes not that cute, animal-guests: ducks, wild rabbits, squirrels, ravens, and once a rat. I felt like Snow White in the forest, surrounded by all the wild creatures – except that, unlike Snow White, I was living in a rather central location in the second largest city in Denmark.

Speaking of the parks, one of my ever-favourite spare-time activities, when I need time on my own, is to walk around the Copenhagen Lakes or in Frederiksberg Garden and observe the sun shining through the leaves above. I also like to try to capture it with my cell phone. I am embarrassed to admit how many times I have tripped because of walking with my head tilted up to the sky.

Not being able to imagine life without 'hygge'

'Hygge' refers to enjoying the simple pleasures of life and the quality time spent with your family and friends, creating a cozy, warm feeling, which Danes call 'hygge'. The great social atmosphere, the feeling of coziness and peacefulness when you are with a close circle of people, feeling safe and sound – I am so happy I've finally found a word to describe this. Now I can't stop using it and I cannot imagine life without it.

Epilogue

Acculturation is probably the most exciting part of the adjustment process, because it goes beyond the initial anticipation of a newcomer. This is the time when you start to appreciate, but also integrate with the local culture – namely the food, music, fashion, lifestyle, traditions, language, and way of living. Most significantly, you realize that you feel protective over the new pieces of culture that have entered your life. However, you do not only want to try them for the sake of experiencing 'new things', as it is during a vacation abroad, but you subconsciously adopt them as part of your way of living, seeing the world, and your international culture. This is the state when you embark on developing a real affection for your new 'homeland'. When I moved to Denmark, I missed my hometown and family (and I still do), and I never believed it would be possible to develop such deep feelings towards another culture and country. I have changed.

I learned that the slow pace of change is rather frustrating, can be lonely and confusing, but without you realizing it, change happens, and it is for the better.

PART TWO: MAKING THINGS HAPPEN

How to get what you want out of your international life: Values, Vision, Goals and International Career

Chapter Six – Practices of 'Going Further'

Vision: Purpose and Goals

Living abroad means facing constant change. As a natural response to that, while coping with culture shock and daily concerns, we can be trapped in a routine, survival mode. Regardless of whether we live in a foreign country or not, the practicalities of life can overload us to such an extent that we forget to strive for real progress.

I have learned that writing down my goals and keeping track of my personal and professional advancement is the best foundation for my development and achieving what I strive for.

What does **personal development** actually mean?

To me, that has always been about maximizing my potential to the fullest – by knowing my purpose and goals in life, by constantly learning, exploring, experiencing, and thus being empowered to work towards them.

I have selected and outlined in this chapters the best practices and methods that I had applied successfully during my experience abroad. I have found these to be crucial in the journey of progress and towards a prosperous international career.

What is the difference between **practice** and **method**?

Practice is a process. It consists of method(s) and respective actions in order to turn an idea into reality, improve skills, or execute a project, for example. The **method** is a tool – it could be a plan, or any device that can serve for a specific purpose. The practice and its method help you develop a Personal Strategy. Like the strategy in the corporate world, it is built up by a vision, as well as a plan of how to achieve your goals. It sets a direction, and consists of guiding principles (in this chapter referred to as practices).

The vision is your personal development foresight, including goals and dreams related to any aspects of life that are of value to you – such as professional, academic and private. The vision is your core purpose and the heart of your Personal Strategy.

This chapter presents the practices, consisting of methods for goal-setting, creating a clear vision, as well as preparing a plan for achieving your goals.

To simplify the process, we will walk through two main consecutive approaches in developing a success (personal) strategy. We will refer to them as the 'outside-in' and the 'inside-out' approach.

The former ('outside-in') starts with collecting information. The logic behind this approach is that you do not know what the key outcome is, and you start from scratch by making research and gathering data, without knowing where such information will take you. In this context, the core, or the outcome we strive for, is building a vision (consisting of defined goals).

On the other hand, the latter ('inside-out') approach, respectively begins with the purpose and key goal(s) in mind, and works its way 'out' towards achieving them. Your vision of clearly set goals is defined, and you would like to have a plan of how to accomplish and sustain it.

The two approaches are inspired by some of the same fundamentals that form vision and high-level decision-making of successful enterprises in the business world. The approaches are, however, designed based on best practices for personal development – to grow, to be passionate about life and to go after what you want. I recommend both approaches are followed through, even if you consider your vision well defined. The reason is that the simple practices will help you reinforce your goals and set a direction.

Outside-In Approach – creating a vision

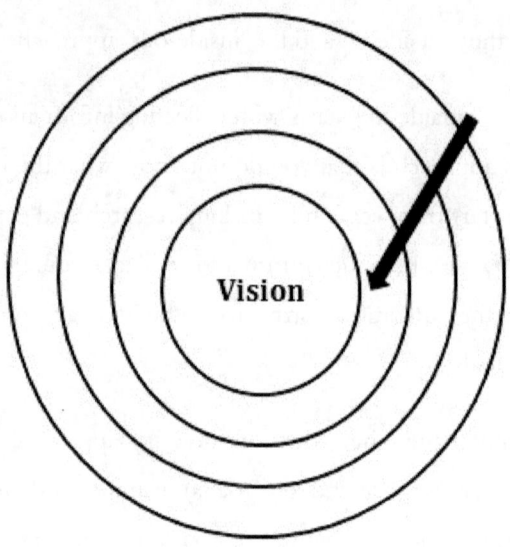

The outside-in approach starts by collecting information on different levels, which help you identifying your vision. There are three essential practices for achieving this.

Practice 1. List your achievements for a definite period

I learned that one of the most important steps of the progress **is keeping track of it**. This practice is effective, since it gives you a holistic view of your development, even if all it seems to be is 'baby-steps'. Keeping track of what you have learned and fulfilled so far, be it during your expatriate journey or career, education and athletic achievements, also serves as an inspirational technique to keep you 'going further'. It is the most empowering tool. Rereading the list inspires you to be able to elaborate on and enrich your pool of accomplishments with new things that you desire to try, work with, learn, achieve, or change. This is simply how you start building own tool towards creating a personal vision.

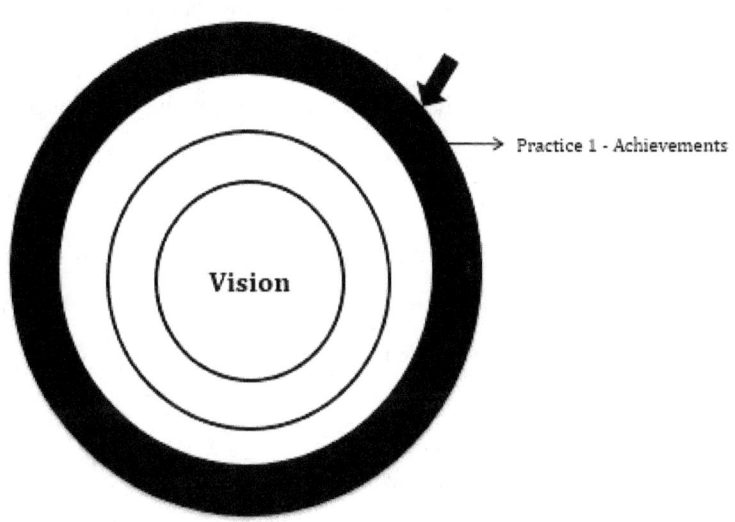

Practice 1: Make a list of all things that you have learned during the past six months (or one year), including anything that makes you proud. If you are living abroad, then you can list all the things you have experienced, including any sort of accomplishments in the foreign country (or countries) you have lived in. It could include anything that you have mastered, learned, achieved, or understood, or that has

brought about a difference in your life – or in somebody else's. Place there all items that you consider significant and meaningful. Overcoming fears should also make the list. Read it several times, and keep filling in everything that occurs to you and that you feel proud of.

Why: This practice will give you an idea of 'where you are', with regards to your personal development. Perceive it as your compass. It will be your reminder of how and to what extent the experience has changed you and what you have learned from it so far. This practice creates an inspirational tool, which motivates you to want a further development and indefinite progress. If you are not satisfied with the items you have on the list, then turn this into your motivational device – a tool that will help you identify what you want to do, change or improve (Practice 2).

How To (Method): To start with, buy a notebook (yes, one made of paper). I always prefer to write goals down with a pen and see my own uneven handwriting, instead of using an electronic document. However, this is a personal choice, so do what suits you best. Just make sure to save the list or document somewhere you can later follow up on it.

In order to give you an idea of what such could contain, I present as an example the list I made when I was nineteen. That was after completing the first semester of my Bachelor's at the Aarhus School of Business. I was officially celebrating six full months in Denmark. For this period of time, I had listed (among others) the below:

1. *Always found ways to help people as far as I can.*

2. *Learned words in Danish.*

3. *Learned how to effectively use laundry, dry cleaner, oven* (please do not judge me, everyone starts somewhere).

4. *Excelled in the ability to run for the bus with a laptop and a 600-page book that was heavy enough to injure someone* (as I said, anything that is out of your comfort zone counts).

5. *Learned to switch from English to Bulgarian, and then to Russian, five times in less than five minutes.*

6. *For the first time in my life, I did subjects like financial accounting, statistics, economics and other completely new courses outside of my comfort zone, and passed all the exams on the first attempt with good grades. Moreover, even if I didn't enjoy some of the subjects, I found out I had a new passion for business, which was growing.*

7. *Became friends with great and inspirational people, from all over the world.*

8. *Found out that no matter how close (geographically) two countries are, there can be a lot of cultural differences.*

9. *Learned that saying goodbye to your significant one in the movies is romantic as hell, but in reality, only hurts like hell.*

10. *Found out that I was braver than I had believed and that, no matter what, I stayed 100% behind what I believed was right.*

11. *Learned to find my way perfectly well in cities where I had never been before.*

12. *Attended costume parties for the first time* (I had always been fascinated by such, just in case you wonder what this item is doing in the list).

13. *Started a student job and become financially independent, self-reliant and able to live by myself 3000 km away from my family – at the age of eighteen.*

14. *Learned to live with a roommate, as well as on my own.*

15. *Worked in a team with people with different cultural backgrounds – and I loved it.*

16. *Learned how to deal with culture shock. Or at least found out that there is such that I had to deal with.*

17. Managed to build my life in a foreign country by myself (but also with the support of my amazing friends that I met in Denmark, and my wonderful friends and family in Bulgaria, who encouraged continuously).

Several more items followed.

If you would like to be even better organized, you can divide the points into categories (University, Career, Relationship, Travelling, New Culture, Languages, Finances, Practicalities, Trying New Things, etc.), so that it is easier to keep track of each area of your life you aim to build upon and enrich. Be enthusiastic about the things you have done, learned and accomplished – I have found out that writing these down on paper gives a strong sense of satisfaction with life and it triggers your brain to strive for more.

Moreover, and even more important, use the list as a foundation to plan your short and long-term goals – what was it you wished had made the list of achievements and experiences?

Practice 2. Prepare a list of the things you would like to do, or do not understand

Subsequently, the next step of your list of achievements is the list of 'gaps'. These form your short-term goals. The list should include all the things you would like to pluck up the courage or find the time to do, learn and improve.

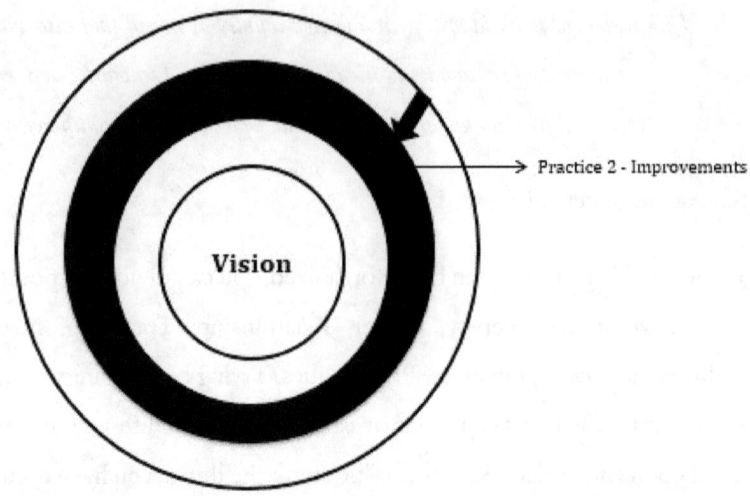

Practice 2: List and critically assess all things you still do not understand, would like to do, or need to improve. Then make a plan of how to find out the answers. It is much easier and more motivating to tackle these when you have them explicitly structured and written down.

Why: Even though acknowledging your personal areas for development is no doubt a less pleasant experience than listing your accomplishments, such a list serves as your 'guidance technique' to critically identify the 'missing pieces' of your progress. It will remind you of what you are aiming for, and thus prevent you from comfortably 'avoiding' the things that need your attention. Such a list of 'needs & wants', including all areas that are not clear to you or that you wish you could accomplish, will motivate you to find the answers and the solutions immediately.

How To: Start by asking yourself the questions: 1) what is it that I wish had made the list of achievements? and 2) what is it that I always needed or wanted to do, but have found excuses not to do (out of fear of failure)? The list should include your needs and wants. Let's distinguish between the two.

NEED: Refers to something that, when present, will increase the quality of your life in a certain way. For example, 'need more experience' in your professional area, or more training in a competence, learning a foreign language, or you may have the need to have more time practising a skill. All these will lead to certain benefits, such as professional advancement, personal development, monetary reward, better social environment and integration, etc., or will increase other people's standard of living.

WANT: Refers to all activities that will increase your satisfaction with life. For example, 'sky-diving' or 'travelling to Japan' can be classified as wants or desires. These are usually initiatives out of your zone of comfort.

The needs and wants often overlap or correlate, so it is not always clear which goal falls into which category. The categorization depends on the individual circumstances, and an activity seen as a must-do for some would not be perceived as a priority by others. However, I recommend you to prioritize based on importance. Needs often score higher on importance than wants. Alternatively, why not work in parallel, if time allows?

There are many ways to create such a tool so that it fits your idea of guidance and action plan. As the example on the next page illustrates, I would structure these items in a table, because I like to write down as much information as possible, but there is no one right way to make the list. The table presents a (brief) proposal with randomly picked examples of how to draft, develop and structure the plan of Practice 2, so that it takes a form and makes sense. It is a simple but effective way to exemplify the method.

NEEDS & WANTS

I would like to:	Suggested Action	Support	Need or Want
Understand Danish	• Sign up for Danish Language classes at (Insert name here) • Watch Movies in Danish (or with Danish subtitles) • Commit to start reading books in Danish	• Ask colleagues to speak Danish to me	Need, because by being fluent in Danish, I believe (for example) that I would have a larger pool of opportunities and easier integration and life in the country
Know how to maintain my own website	• Attend the course on HTML at the university • Research online courses or YouTube videos with explanations	• Contact (Insert name here), who studies Multimedia and Design, and ask for advice	Need, because such a skill will enable me to be independent when there are technical issues with my website

I would like to:	Suggested Action	Support	Need or Want
Become better at Advance Excel (as an example of focus area)	• Allocate three more hours each weekend at reading materials and solving Excel cases • Watch tutorial videos with suggestions for solutions and formulas • Request for a course at my company • Complete an online course at Coursera	• Create a study group, where we can solve cases together, and help each other understand the solutions • Invite a colleague who is an area expert to work with data sets and pivot tables together	Need, because I would be better at extracting data for my analyses at work
Fly with a hot-air balloon	• Investigate the options in Denmark • Check the options outside of Denmark: safety, time, areas, and price • Book the ride!	• Find out if there are any preliminary training courses for taking a hot-air balloon ride	Want

You may optionally also add a deadline to each sub-action, to make them definite. It may seem rather simple, but once these needs/wants are clearly presented, your brain is aware of what you should work at, and what action each calls for. I know it is much easier to make the plan than to start working, but I've learned that if you can write down and then read the goals regularly, you will be more committed towards achieving them.

Where can you get the last but critical component in this practice, namely the *Support*?

Friends and Family

Start with asking for support from your innermost circle. Your family and closest friends will be the first people to get excited about your endeavours, and will give you the most trustworthy advice and support.

Surround yourself with positive, honest, motivating and supportive people, who will encourage you and give you a sincere feedback and guidelines on how to advance.

Communication and Networking

At the same time, be open to networking and meeting new people – especially people who are different from you. The more diverse (in background, skills, interests, career, aspirations, education, culture) circle of friends and contacts you build, the better chance you learn, complement and help each other. Diversity triggers creativity and opens horizons. By knowing people, who have different career and interests, thus knowledge and expertise, I have discovered that I can learn, try and do new things every day.

Many people have difficulties getting in touch with different-minded individuals. Join organizations, forums and conferences. Start conversations and talk to people first. Respect each other's contrasting traits. Otherwise, you do not allow yourself to get out of your comfortable world – and why stay there, when you could have a great one with amazing and inspiring people in it.

Think about the people you would like to meet: what groups, organizations or clubs are they part of? Apply for these organizations and networks (tip: LinkedIn will help you out find out about many exiting events in your area), or if these are not open forums, ask for an invitation or a recommendation to join, online and offline. I recommend you make a thorough business LinkedIn online profile, if you do not have one already. From my experience, joining this online network (and using it) is something you should consider to increase your chances to be noticed and contacted by prospective, interesting business contacts.

Join communities and network events, even if you think you are too busy for such extra-curriculums. Networking is crucial for gaining valuable insights, knowledge, information-sharing and socializing abroad. I have learned that asking for advice comes in incredibly handy.

Books

You might think that reading books is a rather *passive* method of finding real support, but advice and lessons written down by experienced people are one of the most valuable forms of support I have received. Read books. Because indisputably, they shape readers' lives. How to find them? To start with, you can take a look at the listed further reading for inspiration I have selected at the end of the book, and then pick up what you consider the most relevant/ helpful/ inspirational material. Besides my family, friends and colleagues, these books (or more concretely, the experience shared by the authors) have shown me the 'light in the tunnel', not only for career-related concerns, but also for life matters in general. You can also try search for *'the most inspirational books of all times'*, if this is what you need.

Online Courses and Channels

YouTube contains a considerable amount of tutorials for different practical and technical issues, made and uploaded by professors from all over the world. It is as simple as that. Such lessons have helped me master my Excel skills, recap SPSS (statistical program for quantitative data analysis) and find inspirational cooking materials (for my friends and my fantastic boyfriend, not for me). YouTube has a wide variety of content but one of the aspects I have found most valuable are such tutorials.

Have you heard of **Coursera** (https://www.coursera.org/)? The platform offers higher education courses from top colleges and universities, for a rather modest fee, in diverse fields such as social sciences, business, innovation, strategy, economics, finance, life science, engineering, arts, programming, and many more.

There are also some universities that provide courses for free – I recommend you check out the website called **Academic Earth** (http://academicearth.org/), for example. Moreover, the **University of People** (http://uopeople.edu/) gives tuition-free, accredited online academic courses and higher education.

For inspiration and provoking one's brain, I also recommend you look at the below websites:

TED videos (http://www.ted.com/): I sincerely hope you have at least heard of it. If not, I suggest you search through the wonderful videos featuring talks on interesting perspectives about all sorts of topics.

99U in YouTube (https://www.youtube.com/user/99Uvideos): This is streaming, displaying fascinating ideas on entrepreneurship, productivity, leadership, innovation and more.

Brain Pickings (www.brainpickings.org): Online world corner for curious people craving knowledge, food–for thought and new ideas within art, design, history, anthropology, psychology and much more.

I strongly recommend you to also join/follow relevant groups, organizations and discussions on **LinkedIn**, as I briefly mentioned previously.

Practice 3. Make a 'Dreams Plan' for Long-term Goals

So far, you have created a detailed list of achievements, followed by all aspects you wish you could do, learn and improve on (short-term goals). Hence, we are reaching the next level of creating and sustaining a personal vision – long-term goals and dreams.

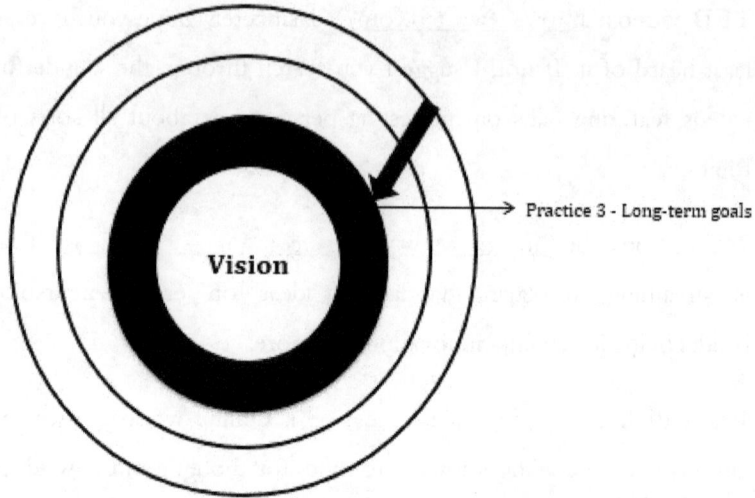

Practice 3: Make a thorough list of your dreams. This should be the third page in your notebook or electronic file. Translate these dreams into organized thoughts, and place them on blank sheet of paper/document.

Why: Self-motivation is the biggest and the best driver for progress, and sincere personal dreams and goals are what nourish the inner motivation. Therefore, built upon the previous two practices, the creation of a 'Dreams Plan' represents the third tool of your improvement and development plan.

How To: This plan requires more solid consideration and preparation. Therefore, I suggest you construct it by the following step-by-step method.

Step 1. Brainstorming

Start from the basics – imagine where you want to be and what you would like to be doing in one or two (or five?) years, in all areas of your life. Build the illustration in your mind, as you imagine everything the way you want it to be, not the way you think is 'most realistic'. Then write down all keywords, describing your ideal life, no matter whether they are nouns, verbs or adjectives. The list can be something like: *Entrepreneur, National Champion in karate, Author of a bestseller, speak fluent Spanish, live in Barcelona, graduate with a Master's degree/MBA, have a fitness certificate in Personal Training, visit my family in (Insert a country here) more often.*

Practise this exercise as many times as needed, to allow your brain to locate your most desired goals, and update the list with keywords until you consider it as completed as possible.

Step 2.1. Categorization

After you have found out the keywords of the most desired long-term goals, and thus have identified your dream-roles, you need to put the goals into perspective. This means 'fueling' these dreams by actual planning by the help of categories. The categorization needs to incorporate as a minimum these four groups: *Required Actions, Resources, Timing, and Occurrence.* You then have to elaborate on each, by doing research or asking for a support, in order to allocate all information you need.

Required Actions category must contain all activities and tasks you believe you need to engage with, to achieve the goal.

Resources should critically assess what is required, in terms of support, capital, knowledge and tools.

Timing is where you should realistically give yourself a timeframe, thus making the goal definite.

Occurrence gives a sense of whether the goal is an 'ongoing' event, which you would like to re-occur, or a one-time goal. An example of an 'ongoing' dream is *'to become entrepreneur and manage my own start-up'* or *'visit my family more often'*. Such a goal requires ongoing actions and indefinite commitment to sustain it. On the other hand, an example of a one-time goal can be *'to graduate with a Master's degree'*, since such a goal demands actions which will be limited in time, until the goal is fulfilled, i.e. with the receiving of your Master's diploma.

Here is what such a plan can look like (as a start):

Making Things Happen

Goals	Actions	Ongoing	One time	Resources	Time
Be an Entrepreneur	• Make a business plan for your ideas	✓		Financial investment of (insert amount)	1-5 years
Write a book	• Start brainstorming • Make a draft of chapters and topics		✓	Allocating time Professional editing cost	1-2 years
Speak fluent Spanish	• Sign up for Spanish language classes during the weekend	✓		Fee for the courses	2-3 years
Live in Barcelona	• Research the cost of living, job opportunities, finding apartments	✓		Allocating time Cost of living	NA
Receive a Master's degree	• Research the Universities in Spain/Barcelona		✓	Tuition fee	1-2 years
Have a certificate in Fitness	• Save up and sign up for the three/four weeks course		✓	Course and certificate fee	3-5 weeks
Visit family more often	• Travel home every two months, buy tickets in advance, plan ahead, etc	✓		Vacation and travel planning	Every two months (ongoing)

Step 2.2. Interconnection

Once you have brainstormed and categorized all your goals and their prerequisites, you should come up with a plan of how to interconnect these goals as much as possible, so that they can mutually re-enforce each other.

Let us reflect upon the above, in order to illustrate how such planning can be thought of.

First, I would place *'Visit family more often'* as a top priority, since it is an ongoing goal, and because being with my loved ones, and maintaining healthy family relationships for me is the most important. You can structure and prioritize these in very different ways.

In order to correlate the rest of the goals, you have to think in a way, *'which can affect what and how'* in the most resource-efficient (time, capital) way. There could be several possible scenarios, but I will illustrate one example and way of thinking about the correlation. Wherever possible, your actions should be linked in a way that they work for each other, at the same time. Such planning is solely based on your assumptions and priorities.

I would do my best to find a Master's degree in the country where I consider having my future career realization. If I already know that I would like to live in Barcelona and to pursue a Master's degree at the same time, then my most logical course of action would be to prioritize finding the right degree and university in Barcelona, or at least within the borders of Spain. Thus, I will focus on being admitted to an elite level and affordable university, where I would be happy to pursue a degree. This way, phase 2 and 3 will be fulfilled simultaneously.

Once I move to Barcelona, I imagine it would be much easier to learn and practise the language. Therefore, *'speak fluent Spanish'* would be phase 4. By acquiring a higher education and learning the local language, I would therefore also indirectly be working towards my goal of becoming a manager of my own company. This is so, because I would believe that local knowledge, gaining expertise and speaking the local language play an important role in establishing one's own business, expectedly.

After gaining experience in the new country and new position, I would expect to be more prepared to write a book, since I would have gained the experience and valuable knowledge to be able to tell a story (for example). Finally, I would place '*acquiring a certificate in fitness*' as a last point, since (I assume) it usually takes several weeks (or more) to complete the training and can be done basically at any time or in parallel with my other goals, as long as I have decided to allocate time and energy for it.

Thus, ideally and very simply exemplified, this is how I would have mapped and structured such actions related to the above goals.

	Goals	Actions	Ongoing	One time	Resources	Time
5	Be an Entrepreneur	• Make a business plan for your ideas	✓		Financial investment of (insert amount)	1-5 years
6	Write a book	• Start brainstorming • Make a draft of chapters and topics		✓	Allocating time Professional editing cost	1-2 years
4	Speak fluent Spanish	• Sign up for Spanish language classes during the weekend	✓		Fee for the courses	2-3 years
3	Live in Barcelona	• Research the cost of living, job opportunities, finding apartments	✓		Allocating time Cost of living	NA
2	Receive a Master's degree	• Research the Universities in Spain/Barcelona		✓	Tuition fee	1-2 years
7	Have a certificate in Fitness	• Save up and sign up for the three/four weeks course		✓	Course and certificate fee	3-5 weeks
1	Visit family more often	• Travel home every two months, buy tickets in advance, plan ahead, etc	✓		Vacation and travel planning	Every two months (ongoing)

Always bear in mind that these change a lot due to your career preferences, new goals and ideas, priorities and more. My real list is longer, very flexible and dynamic, because I add new goals to it all the time.

Step 3. Positive Attitude

Finally, think positively. I know it sounds easy to say; the obstacles are hard to ignore. However, this is your story, and you must think with certainty. Positive thinking is the last piece that will keep you 'moving' when it is difficult, or it is taking a longer time than you anticipated. I have learned though that the world can offer me everything, once I have it clearly stated and visualized, believe in fulfilling it and I am willing to work for it. When I approach situations with a *positive attitude*.

Do not leave the well-thought plan as a static document, but turn it into a map of what to work for. In order to be able to do that, you have to think of it as an aptitude, which will help you live your goals. Why is positive thinking a real talent and skill? Simply because, as with every ability and competence, you should *practise* it. We often tend to be critical and negative when it comes to our goals, out of fear not to have too high expectations and end up being disappointed.

Here is my suggestion how to practise and develop a positive thinking and attitude.

Imagine a situation with two scenarios and two possible outcomes

Let's visualize that the situation you encounter is introducing yourself to a group of people or a person whom you admire, and you happen to be at the same (networking) event together. It could be a conference, a party, a symposium, or similar setting. Let's build two hypothetical scenarios of the case.

Scenario 1. Imagine you approach this circle of people with the attitude that they will probably not be interested in talking to you and that you are going to feel embarrassed or waste your and their time. What do you think is going to happen in this case? Even though your hypothesis would most likely be far from the truth, you would be nervous and seem so shy and negative that you would appear as if you have no desire to talk to these people. Not because you are not 'interesting', but because you *yourself* would choose not to seem easy-going, open-minded and positive.

The alternative is that you do not pluck up the courage to talk to the new people/person of interest at all. I have learned that attitude is crucial. You would be surprised to find out how this subconscious thinking changes your confidence and appearance, and impacts on people's attitude towards you.

Scenario 2. Imagine you have an extremely interesting conversation and make at least one good contact out of the new experience. Think of all the things you would like to ask and discuss. Then prepare yourself to *listen* more than talk.

From my experience, most often the only obstacle that would have made a difference at the end, when everything else was in its right place, would have been my attitude towards the problem, goal or any event. I have found out that the best I could have done was to believe in the positive outcome and ask the question, *'what is the worst that can happen anyway?'* Thus, looking back, what I have wished for or have regretted after an occasion that had not worked out, was that I could have been more positive about it.

When I was still at the beginning of my education at university, I found it hard to be truly satisfied and at peace with results. This starvation for achieving more was affecting my 'positive attitude' negatively. I wanted to accomplish simply everything I put my mind into, and in a perfect balance, ticking off checklists, trying to save and help everyone, while also excelling at everything… I was never fully satisfied – it was never good enough.

As a result, I decided that I had to stop torturing myself, but instead turn my head to everything positive in my life, and to start noticing and appreciating the 'small' steps forward.

Here is how: I discovered Practice 1, i.e. listing everything I had learned and achieved, in order to create a sanity check: was I on the right track? Was I happy with the achieved? Then, I created the habit to re-practise Practice 1 regularly. What we usually forget is to give ourselves an appraisal and credit for our achievements – did they make us happy, were they worth the effort, time and energy, did they make a difference for us or somebody else? I have learned that such assessment is vital, since it gives us a clear idea of what we are still missing (hence supporting Practice 2) and also guides us to what our vision/goals are (Practice 3). When I do this evaluation, I occasionally find out that some of the things I so desperately wanted to achieve, were not that important, after all. This is so, I have learned, because we cannot, neither should we, strive for perfection or for excelling at everything. However, we should strive to find what we need and want to do the most, and work towards developing and improving in that area.

The above illustrated tool is far from the only or the optimal way to construct and develop your Dreams Plan. I have followed the above matrix, but I have found out that goals do not always correlate – often they go in very different directions. In any case, create a new plan for each of your goals. For example, your career would be something that would require separate action planning (see Chapter 7).

Your plan is a dynamic tool, which requires constant reflection, regular 'going back', rereading and rewriting. This is very intuitive but is still important to mention, since, from my experience as a mentor to foreign students and graduates, many people neglect the importance of follow up and time management. At the end, managing time wisely, and thus putting the commitment of time and engagement into action, following up and reflecting, would be the final and crucial step, in order to turn their plan into reality.

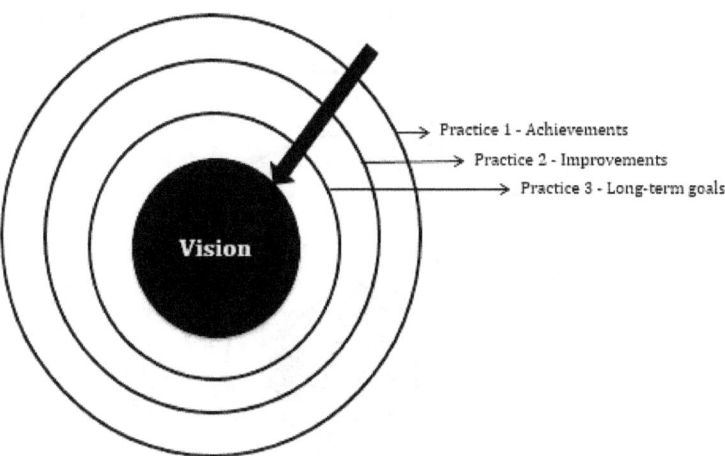

The power of these three practices helped me determine what I wanted – out of my international career and out of my life abroad, and they pushed me to work for it and accomplish it. The next approach illustrates how.

Inside-Out Approach – when you have a clear vision and would like to achieve it

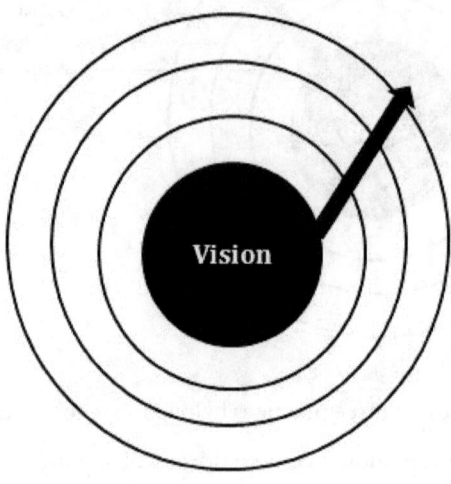

The inside-out approach starts by having a vision - purpose and goals in place. There are three essential practices for achieving them.

After setting clear goals, making an action plan and defining a direction, we need to outline the way ahead. This is what the 'inside-out' approach is for. With the main outcome (vision) in mind, you prepare a plan for achieving it. I have highlighted the three main pillars you need to identify, in order to live your vision.

Practice 1. Identify Main Values

This is as crucial to the development of your Personal Strategy as it is for an enterprise when developing their Business Strategy. Why? Because values are our core guiding principles – they set a direction, influence our perceptions, mindset and the way we act. We all possess underlying values, which motivate us in our daily lives and define the drive and attitude we have towards various situations, problems and our goals. These underlying principles also affect how we view the world, including the very fundamental things such as what we eat, what motivates us, or how empathic we are. We also use values when making judgments – often not consciously. Therefore, I chose to place the values in the inner circle, closest to the vision and purpose.

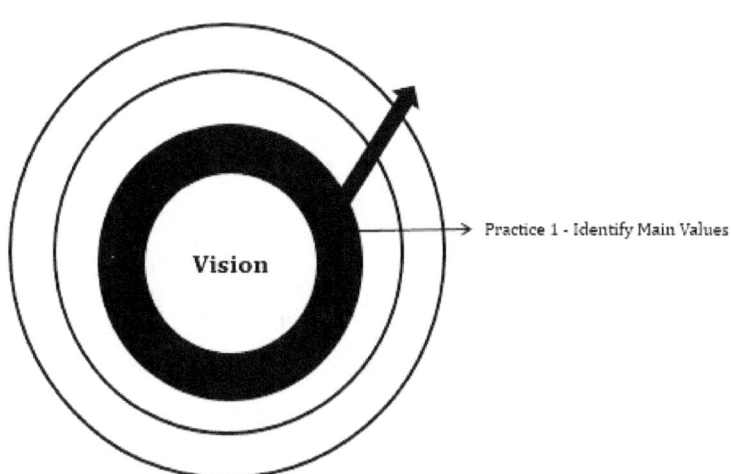

Practice 1: The approach starts with identifying your values.

Why: When you have a concise vision of what you want to achieve and where you want to be, the values can tell you a lot about your self-direction, perceived limitations, motivation and prioritization in life.

How To: Namely, you need to be able to answer the question:

What beliefs and behaviours will guide me in achieving my goals?

'Values' are abstract. Therefore, answering the above question is harder than anticipated, which is why I will guide you by the following example.

When making this exercise, I divided the question into the following categories:

1. Beliefs (Aspirations, Interests)

2. Mission

3. How I want to make a difference, expressed in:

    3.1 Nouns, 3.2. Verbs and 3.3. Adjectives, and

4. Personal values

Next, I made a brainstorming exercise with myself and started filling in all categories and sub-categories, by linking them to my vision. For the purpose of this example, I used one of my goals: to be a leader and an influencer. Not necessarily in a corporate context, but a leader in a way that I would like to be able to influence, help and inspire millions of people in achieving their dreams. Therefore, my main principles can be broken down to:

1. Main Beliefs, Aspirations and Interests

I believe that I am honest, direct and trustworthy, and I concentrate my efforts to fight discrimination and to bring more open-mindedness, morality and righteousness in the world.

I stand for equality and anti-discrimination on gender, nationality, ethnical background, etc., and I work towards achieving it.

I would like to work with respectful, honest and cooperative people, who have integrity and empathy, in an international, multicultural, cooperative and non-discriminative environment.

2. Mission

I would like to share information and create knowledge for people on how to find our place and purpose in the world, without being constrained by national or personal boundaries.

3. *How I would like to make a difference:*

3.1. *(IN) Nouns: Life of others (by means of) strong drive, solid can-do spirit, empathy, integrity, knowledge-sharing and inspiration.*

3.2. *(BY) Verbs: Sharing lessons learned, striving to help others, creating clarity in my area of expertise, exercising leadership, bringing more beauty in the world, motivating and inspiring others to set and pursue goals, be determined and go after what they want in life.*

3.3. *(BY) Adjectives: (Being) the best person I can be: supportive, helpful, loyal, positive, thoughtful, persistent, honest, kind, noble, fair, assertive, committed, brave, determined.*

Even if most of your values are concerned with the well-being of others, subconsciously you also bear personal values that are related to self-achievement or self-enhancement. These are driven by a strong desire for outstanding personal results (academic, business, entrepreneurial). For example, even if your business idea is related to improving the standard of living of others, if successful, it also brings positive results to you, even if it is not acknowledged as a main motivation. Nevertheless, these also form your values-system. They can be: decision-making power, individual recognition, publicity, fame, financial stability. I decided to call them *Personal*. These can often be the values that we do not want to admit to openly, but that are fundamentally part of our value-net.

Even though personally I can see that most of my values are related to helping others, I am aware that I am also very self-reliant and individualistic, competitive, and strive for out-performing in related areas. Personal leadership is not shameful; be open and honest to yourself about it.

Therefore, I included the last category:

4. Personal values

I also value the ability to be recognized as outstanding, bright and talented in my fields of expertise and interest. I would like to stand out, have the courage and opportunity to be in the spotlight, and for my greatness to be seen, rewarded and appreciated.

There. I said it (or wrote it down).

This is one way of mapping your values in several categories. These core values should serve as guidelines when reaching your goals. They are the foundation and backbone of your vision. Clearly defining them would explain your frustration, for example, with a given situation and why you have strongly perceived it as unfair. Instead of forming constraints, your values are doing the opposite: they are empowering your goals, because you would know exactly what you are looking for, how you would like to feel, and what you cannot compromise with. Choose values that support you.

Practice 2. Identify 'Key Factors for Success'

After being aware of your core values, the second practice in the inside-out approach is to identify the prerequisites that you consider for reaching your goals.

Practice 2: Identify 'key factors for success': what are the factors that can have a significant impact on your vision and its success?

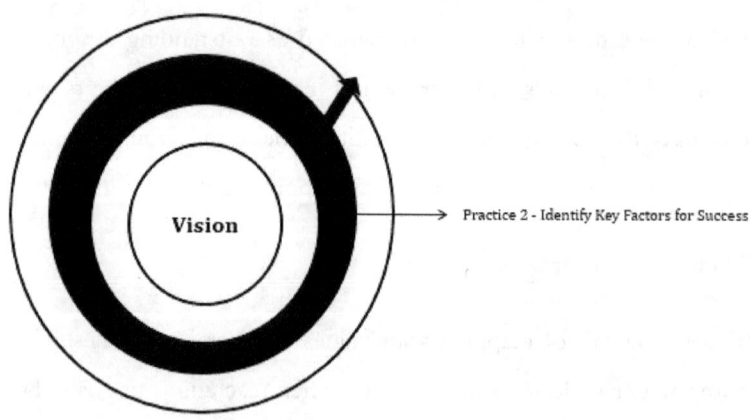

Why: These are the factors that:

If not managed, would hinder your goal, or:

Without having these in place, the goal cannot be accomplished.

How To: There is no one best universal way to map your key success factors on which your goal is dependent. However, it is important that you prioritize them, and subsequently link an action and timeline to each main factor – what can you do to make sure these will empower your goal, instead of posing a limitation?

You need three basic steps when identifying the key factors:

1) Identify the main prerequisites in a random order, per goal.

For example, these can be sample factors someone can consider important prerequisites for starting their own venture:

INVESTMENT   PUBLICITY   SUPPORT TEAM

CREATIVITY   TRAINING

2) Prioritize the success motivators.

I recommend you ask and answer with ✓ (standing for YES), X (for NO) or with ? (for not sure/don't know) as a minimum the below three simple questions, by relating them to each factor:

1. *Does this factor hinder or support my goal?*

2. *Does this factor save me any money?*

3. *Does this factor save me any time?*

As some of the motivators may be hard to measure 'in advance', you may have to answer with an estimate, based on the best of your knowledge and belief. Make assumptions. At the end, arrange the factors in a priority order, where the factor with the most 'ticks' should be priority 1, and subsequently ranked by decreasing number of items answered YES. To make things simple, factors with equal number of scores should be ranked the same priority. The factors with '?' can be left at the bottom as such need more time to assess. The evaluation is subjective and approximate, but will help you discover your priorities.

Example of Prioritizing.

Priority	Does this factor hinder or support my goal?	Does this factor save me any money?	Does this factor save me any time?	# of ✓
1. Investment	✓	✓	✓	3
2.1. Team	✓	X	✓	2
2.2. Training	✓	X	✓	2
3. Publicity	X	X	✓	1
4. Creativity	?	X	X	0

Finally, it is highly recommendable if you are able to quantify the effect of each factor (How much time? What amount? Etc.), or to elaborate where and how it can support your target, by adding extra columns: *'In which way?', 'Why not?'* and *'How much?'* You can build upon the existing table as you like, as long as it works for your purpose.

3) Add an action and a deadline to the priority factors.

I would expect that, in reality, you would have identified perhaps at least ten factors for success to work with. Select only the ones that have the most ✓ (top 4-5) and start with them. Add actions and timeframe. Sample of action and deadline setting can be:

Priority	Actions	Due
1.Investment	1. Save (Insert a number) amount per month	In 12 months
	2. Find sponsors	In 6 months
2.1.Team	1. Evaluate how urgent it is to form a team	Short-term ASAP (as soon as possible)
	Target relevant potential team members (via network events, social media, cold emails, etc.). What is the value proposition to them – i.e. why should they be involved in the project, company or idea?	In a month
2.2.Training	What type of training do I need to succeed and achieve the necessary progress? Who can provide such?	Short-term ASAP (as soon as possible)

The table gives an example of an overall, high level action-setting to tackle the main factors you would be dependent on. Most likely, some factors would require a more profound action plan itself, depending on what your desired outcome is. If you need an investment to start your own business abroad, then you might need to consult with local tax authorities, prepare a business plan and pitch it to investors.

Practice 3. Identify (Additional) Resources

Last, but surely not least important, and closely linked to the key success factors, is to consider what additional resources you require, in order to achieve your goal.

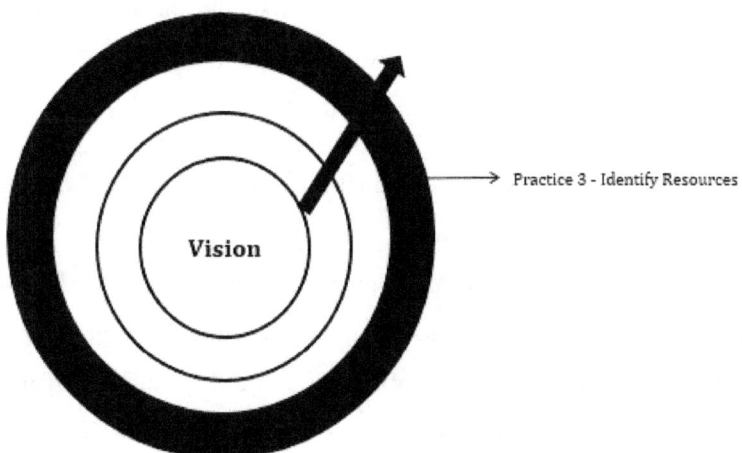

Practice 3 - Identify Resources

Practice 3: Based on your 'key factors for success' list, come up with any further necessary resources or support (additional capital, consulting services, reading material, etc.). Similar to the values and the prerequisites for success, the resources will have to be adjusted and re-adjusted in the process.

Why: Unlike the key factors for success, which are the *must-have* prerequisites for your goals, the additional resources include any tangible or intangible asset you evaluate as *nice-to-have*, such as extra financial help, receiving a career consultation, advice by a life coach, reading relevant books, or getting help from friends and relatives.

How To: As we have discussed the Resources and Support practice in the 'outside-in' approach, I will not go into detail with how best you can identify the resources. However, you should think in terms of *impact* – i.e. what will happen if (insert an element) is absent, and come up with an alternative solution.

As a foreigner, finding the needed resources can be a bit tricky, given that we often think in terms of limitations: lack of sufficient networking circles, poor local language proficiency, lack of entitlement to local social benefits, etc. However, instead of searching for excuses, we should focus on finding opportunities, with drive and confidence. Focus on what you have and can do and on what you can offer. Innovative thinking and different perspectives? Proficiency in foreign languages? Strong determination? International network? Moreover, I have learned that you can always receive help and advice if you ask for them.

Below is the complete overview of the 'inside-out' approach for going after your dreams and moving towards your goals.

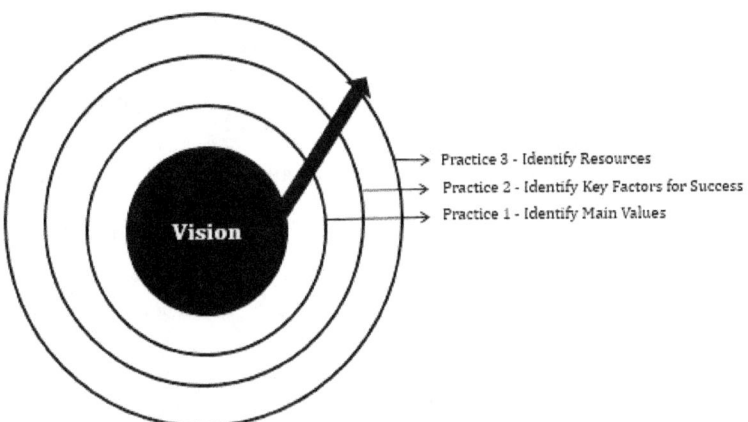

What if things are still not happening?

What do you do when you have the vision – defined goals, an action plan in place, and you do whatever you can within your control, but things are still not working out as you wish?

It was not the right time

During the time I was studying for my Bachelor's degree, one of my goals was to be part of one top talents organization, which was an exclusive network for bright and experienced students and graduates. I was very young and inexperienced, but I applied nevertheless – my stubbornness had a confidence in myself, you see. I spent a lot of time preparing for the application process, and had received a great recommendation too. My motivation and positive attitude led the way.

Despite this, I was told that I needed to wait, study and work for some more years, and apply again when I had gained more experience.

They were right. It was not the right time, and I knew it too. Yet, it did not feel good – it always hurts to get a rejection, especially for something you want very much. So, I put this goal at the very back of my head, and off my 'list'.

Unexpectedly, four years later, colleagues, classmates and friends of mine, separately from each other, started suggesting to me how I must apply for the same network. They thought it was something for me. The truth was, I had completely forgotten about the organization. My colleagues did not even know that I had, once upon a time, applied and was told, *'thanks, but no thanks'*. Because it was simply not the right time.

Encouraged by their trust and hopefully good judgment, I applied again and this time got accepted. I was also honored to be invited as a speaker at one of their events.

Therefore, I believe there is a right time for everything, and some goals just take longer time to accomplish. That does not mean that, they will not turn into reality in a couple of years, or why not even several months. They are delayed for a reason.

Some goals prove in time not to be that important after all

You went through fire, travelled to the Moon, came back and turned the Earth upside down, and yet… It is not easy of the assertive, persistent idealist in me to say this, least of all to do – but there might be a goal, which would prove not be worth fighting for any longer. There is a time where you might realize that you should let go, and shift efforts elsewhere. But not before you have tried and done your best first! Take the lessons with you and remember that there are more important things, so move on, and focus your energy on your next dream, because…

When you miss out an opportunity, you do not realize what you gain

Remember the story I shared in Chapter 2 about how much I wished when I was in high school I could train dancesport abroad? Even though that never happened, it opened the door to many other fantastic opportunities – better even. Graduating with a business degree from a top university in the world was only one of them. I learned that some unfulfilled goals are the foundation for something even more amazing coming your way. Stay open for new opportunities, and keep working.

Epilogue

My international life so far has taught me two important lessons when developing a vision: to take chances and to fearlessly go after my dreams.

Therefore, I strongly recommend that you exercise both approaches thoroughly. Spending time in developing a Personal Strategy is no doubt time-consuming, but it is worthwhile, as it gives you:

1. Self-discovery and self-actualization: who you are, where you want to be, what you value the most and what you would like to contribute to the world with.

and

2. Structured, but dynamic action plan of how to achieve it.

Write down your goals. It is your tangible record to refer to over time, which supports you in forming a vision and will also help you evaluate what are the tools to get there.

Chapter Seven – International Career Part 1

Dilemmas and Direction

Following an international career as a recently graduated young professional in a foreign country is no doubt challenging. When I graduated university at the end of 2014, I was twenty-three and I wanted everything – the goals that I'd worked and studied for to be accomplished, right away. I aimed for all ideas to turn into reality immediately. Only three years later, I realize how much I wish I knew back then all the things that know now. Therefore, I am going to give you all the support that I can in creating a career plan, as well as advice about what to be prepared for, what to expect, what works and what may not, and how to succeed in the international job market.

Probably you are thinking, '*I don't need to hear another 'success story' of how someone landed their dream job abroad.*' I have realized also that career success stories probably seem one-sided. This is so because they aim to inspire and motivate you; hence the focus is on the positive outcome, rather than the process. As a result, the disappointments before the experience that had led to a 'success story' are usually not featured. The purpose of this chapter is to prepare you for succeeding down the ambitious road of finding your dream job as an international graduate. I hope it motivates and helps you form realistic expectations and give you the courage to go after what you want, despite all obstacles.

When I graduated with my Master's degree from Aarhus University, like every other graduate I was faced with the decision regarding which career was best to follow – not a unique dilemma, as I am aware. It is almost the same choice that we face when graduating from high school.

Career-wise, my tri-lemma was between a business career for a global company, starting my own venture, or doing all that plus going for an industry that had nothing to do with my education, but had a lot to do with my passions. The latter was writing, acting or modelling. My main 'study relevant' interests were Human Resource Management (people development) and Business Development (new markets, product portfolio, etc.) since I'd had some working experience in both fields during my studies. I believe I had the academic skills and fair knowledge in both, but I was aware I could not have everything, especially in the long-run. And I hated it. Luxurious problem? However, the thought that once I chose one of them, I would probably never have the chance for a career in the other field did not leave my mind at peace.

At the same time, I was considering how to combine my passion for having my own company and brand that makes a difference, as well as other aspirations such as starting a blog, writing books and working on volunteer campaigns for child protection and anti-discrimination.

On top of this, I had another life-changing choice to make. After living in Denmark for five years, I had to decide which country to choose for my future career development. Should I stay in Denmark, move back to Bulgaria, or in due course leave Denmark for another country, as some of my international and Danish friends had done? I was going back and forth between options countless times.

I know what is like to be a young, ambitious, motivated and freshly graduated international student, with as much experience as possible besides your studies, in the form of internships, study-relevant jobs, volunteer experience, extra-curriculum activities, and still to initially hit a rock when it comes to pursuing an international career abroad.

To make it easier for you, I will save you some trial-and-error by sharing all the lessons I have learned when looking for the right career path abroad. What does it mean to pursue a career as an international student and graduate?

Lesson 1. Self-discovery is the prerequisite for setting a direction

Many foreign students and graduates in Denmark believe that if you have your higher education from elite university, if you speak the local language well, have acquired relevant work experience during your studies, are self-motivated, and have sufficient networks, you will find your dream job right away. But these factors, despite vital, might not transfer immediately into 'something great'. Freshly graduated, we often miss the most important part – knowing what we would like to do the most and where to start.

When I graduated with my Master's in October 2014, I could not wait to be 'out there in the real world' and to make the positive impact I was longing to. When I closed the university chapter at the end of 2014, I had already achieved everything that I wanted as a twenty-three-year-old, soon-to-graduate student. I had made many dreams come true, I had travelled a lot, had all my higher education from an elite university, graduated within the top of my class. I had wonderful friends, had worked student and study-relevant jobs the entire time, and had a relevant internship in Denmark with a global leading company, in a position with the steepest learning curve possible. During the five-year period, I had managed to do all volunteer activities I wanted to be engaged in, had managed to build a strong and diverse network in Denmark and abroad, while also prioritizing time for my family and friends, and for doing sports.

So, there I was, standing with my newly acquired MSc. (Master of Science) diploma from Aarhus University, a great employer recommendation and an AU Alumni cup[17] for a Master's graduation present. And, not to forget, a burning passion to save the world. Bring it on Denmark, bring it on world! I had many great expectations for bright career… and no idea where to start, nor what to do next.

It seemed to me that I had everything, and yet nothing figured out. How frustrating! My first thought was that I had to find out what I had done wrong, and fix it. What have I missed?

For the first time in my life, I was replaying in my mind the past couple of challenging years over and over again, backtracking and *trying to find a gap* in my plan – anything that I hadn't done right. There must be something that I had missed, I had thought. I felt as if all I had been doing was putting effort, but the expected After-Graduation clear plan and fantastic future seemed to be delayed somewhere, somehow.

My main motivation behind the extra-curriculums, student jobs and business degree, had not been for the sake of 'getting my dream job fast'. I have always been driven by having a clarity and direction, and for making some positive difference in everything I do. 'Everything' was influenced by gaining experience, trying new things, and constantly learning. Nevertheless, when the time to graduate came, and thus also the time to find out my 'real purpose', I thought that all

---

[17] Alumni gift from Aarhus University, given by the Dean to all Master's graduates at the official AU Graduation Ceremony.

the effort and hard work must lead to something amazing right away. Therefore, I did not just want any opportunity – I wanted the most appealing and exciting one, and the possibility to choose! I was extremely picky, and I was holding my breath, because I believed that great things should happen right away. But how could they, when there was no clear vision?

While trying to make up my mind, I secretly admired all my Danish and international friends who had left the country right after their graduation – to travel, to explore, to work and live elsewhere. It seemed from the outside that they had things figured out very fast. Part of me also wondered secretly whether I had made a mistake by choosing to stay in Denmark. As if leaving would have magically solved everything, and given me a direction. And for the first time, another feeling tried to grow inside me – doubt.

Shortly before my Master's graduation, one of my friends and I discussed the fact that there seem to be many international graduates, who struggle to kick off their careers abroad. Then my friend popped out a question, *'I know you have your whole higher education there (Denmark) and experience, but have you considered looking for a career outside of Denmark, as many of your friends did? Isn't it something that you may want? What are you so sticky about this grey country?'*

No no no no no no no no no no.

'*Yes*,' I replied. Liar.

What if it was an idea worth considering? I had managed successfully to find my feet and fall in love with one foreign 'grey' country; why not manage to do it again? Especially considering I had received offers from several places across Europe.

At the same time, I hated it when people called Denmark 'grey' or 'boring', I was surprised to discover how protective and defensive I felt.

'What about the opportunity you got in Hamburg?' my friend continued. *'You know, it is like being with one leg in Denmark.'*

'True,' I replied, *'but I don't want to be with one leg in Denmark. I want to be with two legs in Copenhagen!'* Who was I kidding? I knew the answer in my guts all along.

I found out that you should be brave and open up – to yourself. In my case, I had turned down an offer from a global leading company, which was no doubt a great opportunity, but had one big disadvantage – it was outside of Denmark. There was no point to keep fooling myself – apparently, I had known the answer all along. I *preferred* to continue my development in 'grey' Denmark.

Many people thought that deciding to stay in Denmark would be the easiest and most logical choice, because of my locally obtained higher education and established network, and because the country was often rated as one of the happiest countries in the world[18]. However, for me staying in Denmark after graduation was the harder choice. It felt harder than returning home, because I knew staying would require me to keep fighting for everything ahead of me, since I had to convince people to whom I was just another 'foreigner' to put their trust in me and give me a chance.

What matters is that, if you are considering an international career, or you are already working abroad, you will have to face the same choice, and probably more often than you may anticipate. It provokes questions such as: where do you see yourself living – and most importantly, settling? Which language do you prefer to use in your everyday life? And in a corporate environment? Do you consider the experience only as a testing ground for future (career) development or as a way to settle in the country? However, the most important question you should ask yourself is where does it feel *right* – where do you feel happy and fulfilled?

---

[18] World Happiness Reports by the United Nations.

I had an illustration in my head of what could possibly happen next, if I stayed in Denmark. Even though it was not yet accomplished back then, I was extremely impatient and excited to try it.

One dilemma was solved for me. Another one was left to unravel.

What I needed turned out to be three months of entrepreneurship to figure out exactly which career path I most wanted to undertake. Once I admitted this to myself, I felt an unbelievable relief. This period was exactly the 'break' that I took after my graduation. However, it was not really a time off, but an active self-development, self-discovery and a time when I contributed to the establishment of a start-up advisory company, which I co-founded.

Later, three months after graduation, I got the right opportunity, because I was ready and aware of my preferred direction. I realized that I did not have to give up on anything. I found out that with drive and commitment, I could do everything that I wanted: write books, travel, be a goodwill ambassador, build a business career. I chose Business Development and Strategy, for the same reason why I had decided to study abroad. I am inspired by international development and progress, and by the opportunity to make a difference on a global scale and to thrive in international environment.

Self-awareness is the key to making choices. What is meant by this?

Being young, inexperienced and ambitious, we are often in a rush. We do not want to 'waste' any time – but to move, succeed, explore. My fast-paced and restless soul also found it hard to accept that I needed time, in order to discover my direction.

How did I figure it out? I pursued the outside-in and inside-out approach (Chapter 6), and saw where they took me. By building the 'big picture' from scratch.

I considered, what was it that had made me stronger and better?

On the one hand, it was an inspirational activity, and it fed a strong feeling of pride and accomplishment. I could not believe how far I had reached and how much I had changed over the past few years, especially given that everything had been done in the context of a foreign country. After putting it all on paper, it seemed close to impossible. Except that it was a reality, and I had made it my reality.

I was surprised to find out how many 'things' we do not remember or do not acknowledge, unless we place them together on a blank list of paper.

Yet, on the other hand, apart from empowering me, the whole exercise also frustrated me. Seemed like, despite everything, I had not figured out what was it I wanted to do the most.

Admit your strengths and areas for development

Acknowledging personal motivators, strengths and things to change and improve is crucial for successful development. If you are able to admit to yourself all these qualities and areas for improvement you achieve a higher level of personal growth: self-awareness.

For example, when doing this exercise by myself, I was finally able to admit that the constant desire for progression was coming from my restlessness. This side of me cannot find peace without feeling that I am *doing something significant*. I am very fast-paced and want to drive performance forward all the time – and thanks to this drive I usually end up way ahead of things. Dynamic environment gives me energy. Because I cannot stay still. Quite a demanding trait, which my friends, colleagues and boyfriend patiently tolerate.

What I've learned is that I can't live without this trait, since it tends to over-think, over-prepare and over-perform, yes, but is also a critical thinker and pushes me to be better and not give up on my goals. It has always also pushed me to choose the road to the scary but awesome life. On behalf of my dreams, thank you, you reckless and restless drive inside of me. On behalf of your dreams – make sure you are fully self-aware of your sharp edges and of when they are most prominent. This is the only way to make an outstanding action plan of what you can do to improve, or to utilize them when needed. Once you acknowledge them, you also start seeing these traits as authentic and achieve a true self-actualization.

I also suggest that you ask people close to you for sincere feedback on what they consider your strengths, talents, and areas for personal development to be, and always ask for elaboration.

Jasen, for example, had brought up that my mind had the tendency to wander, multi-think and try to solve several problems at the same time. However, he also said that I have always had my feet firmly and steadily on the ground – as long as I knew what I wanted, I was determined to go after it. This meant that despite my mind's tendency to be all over the place (area of improvement), I could manage to be determined and to stay focused on my goals (strength).

Therefore, you can either start or end the exercise by considering the perspectives of the people who know you well enough to provide honest and constructive feedback.

The bottom line is that you should have your personality balance sheet in place, which would be your 'self-discovery' tool – and write goals down. This is how I had proceeded after obtaining an international degree in a foreign country. By knowing everything that I had achieved, as well as identifying the areas where I could develop, I was aware of my potential, and was prepared to face the job market abroad.

The missing piece of the puzzle has been having clear goals and vision. Therefore, I was patient to try new ventures – such as forming a start-up, writing and everything I was longing to do, but never had time before. That was how I found out what I was most passionate about and what was best for me.

Remember that it is a process – I still figure out what I want, every day.

Lesson 2. Take your life mantras with a grain of salt

I have learned the hard way that being too trusting and idealistic can backfire. I have also found out that it didn't all come down to what I had done right or wrong, but to my idealistic expectations.

Let's take a look at the life mantras that we all believe should work (in the ideal world):

1. Great things happen to good people

2. When you want something with all your heart, it will come true right away

3. Everything is achievable if you work for it

4. If you are motivated, your goals somehow always work out

5. If you do things 'right', you will be alright;

I found out that most international graduates who would like to use their knowledge and skills abroad but face continuous obstacles, such as many unreasonable rejections, start deep-diving into their lives in search of something that they have done wrong to upset Career-Karma.

This is a completely normal reaction. When something is not going as planned, your subconscious may push you to re-evaluate your actions. When faced with unjustifiable circumstances, I also tend to dwell on ridiculous and unrelated situations, which I am convinced had led to the unforeseen lack of good luck. For example, I was convinced once that my bad luck in taking care of flowers was a payback since I had not taken enough good care of my cactus-flower (or had taken too much 'care' as it died of over-watering). Yes, silly things like this.

Trying to investigate 'where we have been wrong' is exactly where we are all wrong. It is destructive and unproductive. Identifying the things that you could do, in order to move on, is beneficial. Focus your energy on everything you can do within your control – what is it that you believe you have influence over?

I realized that I had to do exactly that and use my time wisely. That was what got me to: 1) create my own company, 2) have the courage to write a book I'd long wanted to start and 3) very soon afterwards, start an exciting job in a fascinating industry in Copenhagen, within the business area I wanted the most.

Three main pillars to be aware of when going after a job abroad

Firstly, when pursuing your dream job abroad, you must be aware that unfortunately you will meet few people who have poor judgment, based on stereotypes, prejudices and risk-averseness – regardless of how bright you are. Such people judge others based on gender, race and nationality. The good news is that you *do not want* to work in such an environment. You deserve to be appreciated and recognized for your skills, diverse background, personality, integrity, ethics, efforts, motivation and performance, and it is worth the patience to find the right place and team.

Secondly, it is not a secret that some 'open' positions are posted online for applications, even though the hiring manager already has someone internally for the position. Fact. However, the company policy may require that all positions must be advertised, leaving many qualified candidates wondering, '*What is wrong with me and my qualifications that I was not even invited for an interview?*' Do not take rejections personally! Let go, and move on.

Thirdly, as discussed under Lesson 1, many recent graduates are not aware of *what they want to do*. Therefore, they prefer to *go with the flow*. I often hear international graduates stating, '*I am looking for a job, but it does not really matter what it will be exactly, as long as it is study-relevant*'. I realize that what they would like to ensure is staying open for different opportunities. All ambitious people have this fear that they may feel restricted, or miss out on a possibility. I can relate completely. I also see that many believe that they will figure it all out eventually, after going into something less desired.

Ironically, I have found out that this attempt of 'leaving doors open' leaves many young graduates not following their actual passion. Looking for a 'study-relevant' job only means that you have no clue of what type of business, industry or career you want to pursue. Your network couldn't help you much either.

I strongly believe that you should go for only these jobs, industries and ventures that you really *want*. Even if you are not 100% qualified, or the job is not exactly your dream job, you must start *there*, and keep learning and developing, as long as it is related to one of your passions.

All in all, life abroad has its own philosophy, which may not align precisely with yours. Great things clearly will not just happen because you are a great person. What I learned, however, was that life was not a checklist – you can tick off everything on the list, and still not have things figured out right away. It is life as it is, not as it should be. In order to make things go the right way – your way – you have to be self-aware, follow your passion to figure out what you want, and prepare a plan of what you need to achieve it.

'Network is crucially important, and not only in Denmark'

After interviewing many professionals, recruiters, career advisors, students and recent graduates in Denmark, I discovered that the common mantra seemed to be, *'good things happen to those who know the right people'*. Not necessarily, but sometimes true. Everyone will tell you to use your network when you are searching for a new job, aim to start your own business or want to change careers. To translate, network is crucially important, and not only in Denmark. However, how can we as foreigners compete and compare with the 'locals', in terms of networks and valuable connections?

International graduates often believe they have weaker networks compared to native graduates. As someone who had always believed strongly (and naively) that with passion, knowledge, hard work, talent and skills, 'things' happen right away, regardless where you are in the world and 'who you know', I was of course also frustrated. This was the case, even after ten years of dancesport championships, where the philosophy, *'those who have connections are often better off than those who have talent'* was also established. My belief still held, because what I had learned from the sport was that *regardless of all obstacles,* you could always beat the odds. You do not need someone else to hand an opportunity over to you. That is not what a network is for. Instead, use your diverse connections for inspiration, receiving advice, knowledge-sharing, for being your references, and for exchange of ideas. Be open and proactive and connect with people – start conversations, ask questions, search for guidelines, submit targeted unsolicited applications, send cold-emails, find partners.

After all, could we then beat the odds in pursuing careers abroad as international graduates? The answer is yes. It is not my over-positive self speaking here, it is my trial-and-error, dusted-down-and-up-again self. It takes Practice 3 (outside-in approach) at its fullest – establishing a personal vision – when you know what you want, your network is also able to help you. Thus, apparently, the cliché '*good things come to those who wait (do not give up) and know what they want*' is also true. Ah, patience had been the key. The one quality I had always struggled with.

Patience is a virtue

I've said that life is not a checklist, but in case you have the ambition, the skills, the experience and a good network, then you should know that it all comes down to patience and persistence. It is naïve to believe that the best things happen right away – I have learned that they take time.

Focus on working on your Dreams Plan and discovering *what you really want* and *plan how to reach it*. In detail. However, this does not mean that you should lean back and relax, or wait for things to come magically to you, just because you are bright and have done everything right. The take away is quite the opposite – when you have accomplished and fulfilled everything possible within your control, and have a vision and clear goals, then the extra mile comes from *listening to your instincts*, and going after what you believe is best for you (not easiest to achieve!) with patience, planning and persistence.

Believe that someone else's *no* means it was not the right opportunity for you. Learn from the experience and any feedback received and stay focused on your goals. Don't just wait for the right opportunity to come knocking on your door, but with courage and patience search actively for it, while also keep constantly developing (for example, by starting your own company, developing ideas, travelling, attending networking events). Do not allow a temporary lack of immediate success and desired results to discourage you.

If you always strive to be ahead of things, you may find this extremely difficult to come to terms with. Not everyone will be able to see and appreciate your greatness or your capabilities, or to care how fascinating a person you are. However, there will eventually be people who will see your talent, and encourage and motivate you to grow, personally and professionally; and I promise you that sooner or later you will come across such people in the industry within which you want to develop.

Don't compromise your ethics and principles

While you should be open-minded to different values, also such embedded in the local culture, stick to your principles and keep improving and striving for change, if this is what you want. I have met potential employers, who thought that I was *'too active and fast-paced'*. Don't pretend you like lying on the couch, if you prefer doing sports instead, or travelling to distant areas with the Red Cross and saving lives. On the other hand, if you are very relaxed and laid-back, do not try to create a false perception of being else. We all have a unique character and different pace. If potential employers do not like the person you are, then they are not the right team for you.

Besides, what is the worst that can happen if you stand your ground? Not getting hired for a role where obviously, you would feel bored sooner rather than later.

However, in the Danish culture, hobbies and activities outside of work are highly important. In Denmark, work is a part of life, not what people live for, and I admire that. Nevertheless, I also found out that in Denmark, 'too much' proactivity can also display the wrong sort of competitiveness. My first impression was that this was due to the Scandinavian concept Jantelagen (The Law of Jante), which criticizes individual success and promotes the belief that no one should strive to be better than the rest. The value behind this is achieving equality in the society. However, it is still scary, isn't it? Especially when you happen to be outstanding in a particular area. Luckily, this mentality is not that deeply rooted. Even though all Danish colleagues and friends, when asked about the controversial topic of ambition and competitiveness, claimed that the Jantelagen is outdated, they all agreed that the Danish corporate culture is much more relaxed and collaborative, rather than competitive and individualistic.

To conclude: have in mind the local values, but stay authentic. Always. Be aware that if you want to succeed in pursuing an international career abroad, you should know the local workplace culture and the incorporated values (I have learned that, despite the globalized world we live in, these differ significantly, also between industries), but never compromise your personal ethics. Do not fake, pretend, dwell on past disappointments, or try to please everyone.

Be true to yourself, even though good life philosophies do not always work. Having realistic expectations about the world is important to be prepared for 'unfair' and difficult situations when pursuing an international career. Stand up for what you believe is right and keep giving 100% towards making a difference in your life, and in others' lives too. I have learned that great 'things' happen, but only with patience, persistence and the ability to adjust, without compromising your values.

Lesson 3. The world is 'slowly getting there'

Hiring international graduates creates a multinational working culture and a diverse corporate environment. It also significantly increases organizational creativity, optimizes problem-solving, and leads to higher efficiency and innovation. Integrating international talent unlocks an enormous potential for the organizational business – specifically when gaining stronger footholds in new markets, expanding to new segments and attracting a broader customer base. Many growing companies have already embarked the journey!

Regretfully, however, few societies and thus businesses are not 'there yet', despite slowly moving into this direction. This means that, in fact, there are organizations, which are not used to working with international talent, nor are open to looking outside the box and hiring qualified foreigners. I have experienced also that some companies have done significant international expansion and operate globally, but still somehow hesitate to hire international employees. These companies have narrowed their horizons (and thus their development and innovation). But this is not relevant only for the business industries!

Look at the leading actors in the world – the majority are either Americans or British. I wish I could see more international artists take lead.

Moreover, the benefits of diversity are countless, only few of them being: innovation, global market and product expansion, and broader pools of new ideas, all of which are proven to significantly outweigh the challenges (communication noise, cultural differences). These 'perks' are researched and analyzed in many reports focused on the benefits of having multinational teams and on the integration of global talent. In Denmark, for example, there is research in the recent years by Dansk Industri (DI) – The Danish Industry Foundation, and Damvad Analytics. The analysis has found that there are many benefits of hiring international graduates, yet, it has confirmed that many international graduates leave the country after graduation. However, there are also a lot of efforts put into retaining the international talents, and such are evident in the numerous network events organized for expats, as well as in the many positions advertised in English, among other initiatives.

It is a two-way street

Many global citizens perceive being a foreigner as a limitation, often due to an imperfect local language proficiency, a lack of network, not having obtained the higher education locally and so forth. And they tend to focus their thinking and energy on the disadvantages that these barriers pose. You must change your perspective. As a global citizen, you should believe that you are a priceless asset. You very likely know firsthand what it is to work and fight for everything, and to have to prove yourself all the time. Thus, you are brave, determined, driven, persistent, independent, adaptive, open-minded and have built a strong will and character.

Moreover, I often see the talent pool in Denmark divided into 'local' and 'international', but shouldn't the international graduates from Danish universities also be considered as 'local' talent in Denmark? I guess we come as the middle group, which I will call 'locally international'. There is a huge ongoing discussion about the importance of retaining this 'locally international' talent and on focusing efforts on also attracting more international students to the Danish universities.

Well, it does not come as a surprise that the most successful companies in Denmark and in the world in general are those who welcome and encourage diversity and are open for the international talent pool. I talk a lot about the business sector, but diversity brings value everywhere. One of the best dancesport couples in the world – several times world champions – is a Danish-Bulgarian mix. Since teaming up together, Troels Bager (Denmark) and Ina Jeliazkova (Bulgaria) are two of the unprecedented leaders in Latin dancing worldwide. Art, sports, business, movie production, music – regardless of the sector, diversity makes a significant difference. It brings novelty, innovation, beauty and progress. That is how magic happens.

In our vastly globalizing world, businesses or societies not open to diversity are putting up barriers for their development and innovation, and are unlikely to prosper in the long-run, as the pool of customers, suppliers and competitors are not local anymore.

As much as the world is becoming increasingly globalized, it can be argued that it is still largely homogeneous and restricted in terms of openness to international talent and embracing diversity. Hence, it is strategically essential to engage in this process in order to prevent losing the young, ambitious and talented people, who can contribute a lot.

Epilogue

Many people believe that succeeding abroad is all about sacrifices. I disagree. I have learned that succeeding anywhere is not achieved by compromises – it is about having the right attitude, clear vision, self-awareness, drive, and ability to let go. I believe it is a misjudged perception that great results come at the high price of sacrifice. I have found out that goals are achieved by a strong drive to excel, and by patience and concentration. It is about using your time wisely and making sure you are noticed. It is not easy, but do not crash your pity party when things do not go as planned. Do not wait in the corner for things to happen; go after them. Never dwell on the obstacles and do not allow the fear of failure or the desire to feel comfortable overtake the urge to go after your dreams. Dare. Shift focus to going forward. The next chapter – Part 2 – is explaining how.

Chapter Eight – International Career Part 2

Center Stage – How to Stand Out

Part 2 of the *International Career* covers practical tips and lessons of applying for your dream job abroad. All these are building upon the lessons shared in the previous chapter, by giving hands-on strategies of how to get what you want out of the red ocean of pursuing a career abroad.

Lesson 1. Preparation is everything – show your motivation and know how to present yourself

As a side-work mentor to international students and graduates, I have been giving advice to peers about the job search in Denmark and abroad, and I have been revising applications of international students and foreign employment-seeking recent graduates. I have noticed that many graduates struggle to write a market tailored application: referred to as a *'Letter of Motivation'*. I could relate to that completely, since I had been there too – at the beginning of my Bachelor's degree, when I was only vaguely aware of how to create a good, targeted cover letter for the Danish market. I had since discovered from experience, and from receiving career counselling, what makes an application outstanding.

Do not underestimate the cover letter

What I learned as an international graduate in Denmark was that the only successful application was the one you had spent time on *individually, by targeting your competencies to the job-specific requirements*. I guess this does not come as a surprise. However, it may then yet come as one that too many people still do not spend time on each *individual* letter, but copy-and-paste standardized text and hope for the best. The prerequisite for a successful cover letter is tailoring it to the job, by writing a new, motivational, personal one *from scratch* for each position you apply for, instead of pasting in previously written paragraphs about your skills. According to the recruiters and employers I spoke to, not spending enough time and effort on the cover letter is the most common and (guess what?) *obvious* mistake that applicants do. Imagine then what a difference receiving a well-targeted, clearly written and to the point cover letter would make.

By making a new application to target the job that you apply for, in the market you are interested in, you show why you are the right person for the position (and it *has to be* of interest to you, otherwise do not waste your time). You can express yourself by explaining what you can do for the company or organization, but also that you know *what kind of problems (okay, challenges) you are able to solve and are passionate about tackling*. Standing out from the crowd is what matters and that is a certain way to achieve that.

How do you write a cover letter that stands out?

To start with, explain what you can bring to the role. Clearly, and to the point. Begin with the experience you have, how it meets their needs and how you believe it solves their challenges.

Furthermore, there is a lot that makes you special, and these specific traits and strengths have to be pointed out, apart from your education and qualifications.

For example, I had spent one paragraph of a one-page successful cover letter explaining what I had learned from doing sports on a professional level, and how this had contributed to my creativity, drive, mindfulness, discipline and efficiency in everyday life and in a professional setting.

As for positions that require technical capabilities, such as engineer profiles, I would assume that some extra qualities may not be best placed in a letter of motivation, though they are recommended to be included in the resume. I advise you to showcase your 'unique' self and mention your real hobbies, not the activities that you think will appeal to the manager or hiring Director. Even if you cannot see how such are directly related to the position you apply for.

Write down the piano skills, your snowboarding passion, the amateur basketball competitions, about the ski lessons you do every winter, your passion for art, books, adventures and travelling the world, and what you have learned from it. After all, hiring managers, casting directors, agencies, and anyone else you may depend on, are all people, not robots. They are interested and touched by personalities, not just by job qualifications. In Denmark, talking about your outside of working-hour activities would be perceived very positively. In other countries, the requirements can be much more formal.

Moreover, you have a global mindset, international experience and a different background, and these traits are valuable. Therefore, make sure you mention or reflect upon your international experience in your letter of motivation. Trust me, there are amazing people and numerous companies who do not live in a small box but want to explore the world and succeed globally, who value the benefits of diversity, and who will integrate you in their teams. You deserve to thrive around such people, and in such an environment – welcoming innovation, prosperity, creativity and development.

Break the conventional, but without crossing the line

I have read a discussion recently on LinkedIn posted by a recruiter, who was puzzled by receiving a text message from a job candidate. The applicant had requested a meeting to discuss a possible position, and to convince the recruiter why she or he was the best candidate for the job. Since the recruiter was based in Copenhagen, I could not help but be curious to find out how the rest of the network views the situation. The plain fact the recruiter had posted the discussion to the open clearly meant that they were uncomfortable by such breaking the rules attitude. Nevertheless, there were many comments from fellow recruiters who strongly supported the candidate's approach. Most people believed that taking the initiative, as long as you are *well prepared* and *professional*, comes a long way.

There is a borderline of course as to being creative by challenging the conventional thinking and processes, and appearing too needy. Do not be too eager or annoyingly persistent by constantly calling or emailing recruiters, instead focus on what you can do to help them succeed and prosper.

How do you stand out during an interview?

As I have hopefully convinced you why you should spend a considerable amount of time on writing a targeted cover letter, I will give you another example and firsthand advice regarding the next step of any hiring process – the interview.

The (first) question, which all of you would probably have at the start of an interview, would be to introduce yourself. It is often referred to as the 'elevator' speech – the ability to present yourself for a period of between thirty seconds and one minute. From my experience, what most international candidates do is to give a speech about where they are from, how old they are, what they have studied, where, and what they have done during their professional experience in the past. That is good, direct and true, but not enough, and most likely not what the people 'on the other side of the table' won't already know. Despite being accurate, the description does not actually present the person you are, neither does it tell your complete story but rather repeats statements from your curriculum vitae.

Since you have been invited for the interview, the recruiting committee will have hopefully already read your resume, thus know what you have studied and where you have worked. Besides that, imagine that all other invited candidates probably have similar levels of education and experience. Therefore, your elevator speech is the perfect time for you to show your trademark. What differentiates you from the rest? Why are you motivated to take on the role?

There is no one universal way to answer the 'Tell us about yourself' question, and I would give you one example from my experience. While finishing my Master's and final project, I had applied for a Graduate Programme in a global company in Denmark. This was an elite two-years programme, which aimed to prepare graduates for becoming company leaders. I was up against at least 3000 candidates, and I was selected for the interview. I was told that I would be given three to five minutes to present myself, and I was well aware that the recruiters already knew my qualifications. There was no doubt that the other candidates would also have good academic credentials, relevant experience and extra-curriculum activities.

Therefore, I decided that I could use these three minutes to show *who I was as a person* in an eye-catching, yet professional way, and not just make a generic and boring description of who I thought they wanted to hear about.

Why do I emphasize *professional*? Well, because if I had to present myself normally, I would just do it this way:

I am a fitness, sports, and coffee aficionado, who loves eating chocolate with a spoon from the jar (more often than I like to admit). I am a person, who is passionate about changing the world, and fighting against any form of unfairness and discrimination.

This was extremely incomplete and brief, but a very honest description of me in thirty seconds, i.e. the perfect elevator speech. However, what would the company do, exactly, with this useless information? Accurate or not, it is lacking a lot of relevant facts. By such details, I refer to any job-related and significant experience. It is the same as when you audition for an acting role or a commercial. I would leave my potential employers and colleagues to find out about my chocolate, coffee and sports addictions later. I am sure they would anyway (it took my new colleagues two hours to figure that out).

Therefore, to prepare a thorough answer, what I did instead was first to map my strengths and passions on a list of paper, which I then used to build my clear personal and professional story. I made sure it reflected my character, instead of preparing a long and unnecessary monologue of my education and experience. As a guidance, I used these three simple questions:

1. *What do I now love doing professionally?*
2. *What am I passionate about in general, in life?*
3. *What are my biggest strengths and core competencies, which would fit the position and benefit the team?*

Therefore, my list of brainstorming (not particularly in any perfect order) was as follows:

1. *What do I now love doing professionally?*

I love taking initiative, setting a direction, being an influencer, leading projects that make a difference (I also gave examples of such), creating more beauty in the world (by means of art, writing inspirational books and articles, participating in commercials, and more).

2. *What am I passionate about in general, in life?*

Sports. I had been doing dancesport professionally, which taught me determination and assertiveness, so I decided to place these qualities in my 'map', even though these were not directly related to the position. I enjoy being active, feeling healthy and fit, and even if these do not have much to do with the job requirements, they have a lot to do with my lifestyle and who I am as a person.

Travelling. Exploring new places and cultures has always been a big part of me and what I strive for. I had also gained international experience by studying in Bulgaria, doing an exchange program in Moscow, Russia and having my higher education in Denmark, and I knew that I most likely also had a different background from the other candidates. Therefore, I decided to touch upon my story of a courageous global citizen, who is self-motivated, and who thrives in an international environment, and knows how to set goals.

Going after my goals and dreams, with a childlike curiosity for learning, trying new things and meeting different people. I briefly mentioned what my aspirations on an overall level were: be an entrepreneur, be an influencer, be a goodwill ambassador for anti-discrimination, be an author (but I skipped some goals, such as my childhood dream to be a detective).

Making a difference in all I do. What has always given me the most energy has been the opportunity to help others, to feel like I have left a mark, and have contributed with what I could.

3. *What are my biggest strengths and core competencies, which would fit the position and benefit the team?*

I have always been proactive in my spare time, and my volunteer experience, I guessed, could speak for itself. However, I wanted to also explicitly present these qualities and not leave anything to 'speak for itself'. If you want to get across a clear and accurate message, you must be explicit. I selected the competences that I believed could best support the role. Moreover, I had some experience and a solid interest in green energy, which was very relevant for the position, which was in the renewable energy industry – so I decided to communicate that in such a way as if it was giving a picture of who I was as a person.

I then made sure that my personal brief story would be presented clearly and would be easy to follow. To do that, I was reading each point from my brainstorming list, and was subsequently asking the '*so what?* questions: '*How does this fit the company and the position?*' and '*Would this skill/trait/knowledge/experience help them and how?*' Anything that seemed irrelevant was left out of the presentation. Moreover, I did a single practice with a friend, to check that my personal story was fitting into three and no more than five minutes.

You should note that, for this specific interview I was given the chance to make a presentation for up to five minutes. In most cases, however, you would have approximately thirty seconds to one minute, without the need of any material. The same tips from above apply, regardless of the time you must fit in.

The result was the following one slide, which I presented during the interview, so that it was easy for the audience to follow my story. Probably it does not give you much, taken out of context, and is far and away not the best way to present your story, but it was a good fit for *me*. Therefore, you need to think always what would suit you; what would most accurately show your personality, combined with what would work for the company.

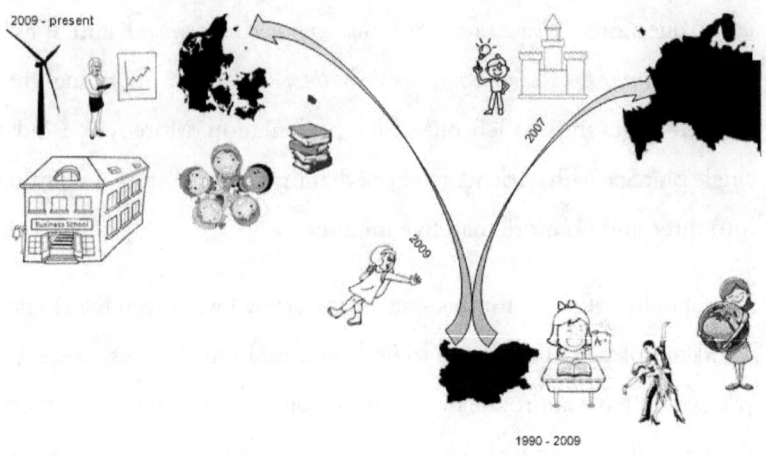

You probably think I am insane to bring such a story to a high-class global leading company, but I did, and I got invited to a second interview immediately afterwards. I strongly encourage you to emphasize on your professional interests, preferences, relevant activities, and your key competencies.

Mistakes at interviews are your pool of valuable lessons learned

I have made many mistakes at interviews during the past five years, which turned into my 'collection' of valuable lessons learned. I had never dwelt on the lack of good performance (regardless of how angry I had been at myself for saying things that I shouldn't have or for not being convincing enough). Instead, I had made mental notes for everything that I could have done differently, so that when I would be given a chance next time, I could do better. Here are briefly some of these lessons:

Do your 'homework' before the interview. Reference to the above story, I assumed from experience that such a rather informal way to tell my story would work in Denmark, and for the organization, due to the down-to-earth corporate Danish culture. Research the organizational structure and find out to what extent their company culture matches your presentation style. If you are still in doubt, get in contact with a current employee there, if you have the opportunity, or even better – ask the recruiter or the hiring manager what their guidance and requirements are.

Do not arrive late. Please. Simply don't. Arrive early if needed, and go take a cup of coffee somewhere, have a walk in the park nearby, wait outside if possible, but never go in late for an interview. As someone who is always punctual, I had the misfortune of arriving 25 min late for a first meeting for a position that I thought was a perfect fit for me. Even though I called the hiring manager to prepare them for the unexpected late arrival, and despite that I apologized many times, as you can imagine, it did not work out. Even if they could close their eyes to my lack of punctuality, I was extremely nervous during our talk, feeling guilty, and my mind was blank, so I couldn't answer even the simplest questions. I did not crash a pity party for a lost opportunity, but I promised myself that this would not be a mistake I would ever do again.

Be prepared for solving cases. Demonstrating how you could solve a fictional case (e.g. business problem) is often a part of the recruitment process. Even if you have extensive experience in solving complex projects, come prepared and do not underestimate this part.

Know your value. Selling yourself short does not feel good. There was a position once, which I fell in love with. The interview went very well (according to my own judgement and their feedback), but then I found out they could not afford to pay me the salary I wanted. So, what do you think happened the next time I was sitting in an interview for a job that I wanted? I lowered my standards and criteria, out of fear for missing an opportunity, and I regretted it immediately. No matter how much you like the position you go for, be aware in advance how much you are willing to compromise.

Do not be afraid to be bright and different

The take away so far is that you have a unique character and background and you must pitch it to the potential investor, agent, employer, hiring Director, or a recruiter you are going to depend on. It requires a profound study of oneself and the job requirements – your career preferences and goals, and what kind of experience, skills and passions fit best your dream job. It is also a fun and essential exercise of self-assessment and self-discovery.

You are not wrong to think differently and to be creative. When I was a kid, I often had moments when I felt uneasy about coming up with ideas that others could not think of. I sometimes even felt concerned that I was having them, and quietly thought that this 'different thinking', which I later found out was referred to as 'thinking outside of the box', was odd. I even wondered whether I should try to hide it. I have learned that you are not wrong to be bright! You are not jeopardizing anything when you are innovative, creative, critical and unique. You are never wrong to be yourself. If you meet people who do not appreciate, understand or welcome the 'challenging of the conventional thinking' approach, it only means that they do not wish to go outside of their comfortable, boring world.

Lesson 2. Proactivity and Passion win over Passiveness

Start with the things you are passionate about

What did you always want to do? Do it now – start your own company, write a book, create your own blog, draw paintings, or do fitness coaching, even if it is on a volunteer basis. Imagine that this period of being 'between university and job' is a unique opportunity for you to work on the projects you never had time for. Such that inspire you, and not only make your dreams become reality but also motivate you and help you find what is the right career path for you. Many of these passions would turn into full-time occupation. The happiest people are those who do things they are passionate about!

I believe Denmark is probably one of the best places to start your own business. The country has been ranked among the best in the world in the category for starting a company, due to the favourable conditions supporting creativity and innovation. Like its Scandinavian neighbours, Denmark encourages entrepreneurship and innovation by funding research and new ventures, creating start-up networks, and many more initiatives, which give a solid basis for entrepreneurs to develop their endeavors.

Regardless of where you are in the world, have confidence in your ideas and in your Dreams Plan. Also, use your time and skills to help others, because nothing can compare to making a difference for people who need it. There are so many options to live your dreams, and many do not require big investments nowadays, with the social media and technological advancements we all know about. They require you to be bold and relentless. Reread and rewrite your Dreams Plan for Long-term Goals at least once per month and do not let life practicalities come between you and your goals. It requires attempt, dedication, desire, passion and persistence.

I always wanted to write a book about the experience of a global citizen, to share the lessons I had learned, because of countless requests for help and advice from expatriates, international students and foreign graduates. I figured that if I'd had these concerns and questions before I had started my education abroad, and if so many other students and expatriates are going through the same issues, there must be thousands of people who have similar questions and interests and would like to know more. However, I never made the attempt until recently, when I just started writing. As I found out, all it required was passion and dedication (and managing my spare time better).

Let me give you an example of a spirit of entrepreneurship, which I admire. Lindsey Stirling – the talented modern violinist, who was rejected by *America's Got Talent*, subsequently conquered the world via making her own YouTube videos, and gradually she became one of the most famous violinists of today.

Clearly all entrepreneurial ventures require taking risks and trying new and different things. With drive and passion.

I have found out that great things happen with a great deal of passion

Complete your Dreams Plan (see Chapter 6). Then place it on your tablet or smart phone, or simply print it out and put it on your desk (very 'old school', but this was what I did, and it proved to be extremely efficient way to get reminded of all the goals I had set), and act upon it. What I learned was that, no matter how smart, exceptional, talented and brave a person is, *things* (career, your goals and dreams) don't usually come along unless you are persistent and 'fight' for them – consistently and proactively. I learned that when you *think* and *feel* that you deserve something, you not only have to work for it, but also *ask* for it. Taking the initiative and developing a great willingness to take the lead and have control over your life is what will eventually turn dreams into reality.

How does this work in practice?

Simply, yet I know also quite challengingly, the answer is – by means of gaining experience. The working experience added alongside my studies played a huge role in my career choice. Dear international students, please be proactive! All-the-time. Studying at an elite university is not enough by itself – you must be active outside of the academic environment, in order to: 1) develop expertise, 2) have a better idea of what you are good at and what you prefer doing 3) be able to stand out when pursuing an international career after graduation and 4) create a bigger network. A busy university schedule is a very lousy excuse. For the record – I have had my highest grades during the periods when I have been most occupied with work and volunteer activities, studies aside. How? You get extremely well-organized and develop a strong sense of responsibility, self-reliance, and proactivity. Being active motivates you to be even better in everything you do. I had found out that proactivity itself is one of the strongest empowerments.

I know that it is tough – and many students comfortably find excuses in language barriers, lack of experience, busy study schedules with classes and exams, etc. Then start with a non-study-relevant job and build it from there, until you have at least gained a certain level of local language skills. Combine the non-study relevant student job with a study-relevant volunteer activity – on campus, online, or elsewhere: there are plenty of organizations, forums and diverse student platforms that are happy to employ international brains and manpower. Then apply for internships – even for those that are for rather short periods, and for internships during the summer breaks. Any experience counts, but if you are planning on staying in your new home country, then you are better off to gain it locally. At least in Denmark, the experience that counts the most is the one received within the Viking land's boundaries.

To wrap up the lesson: regardless of what you have experienced and how unfair the circumstances are sometimes, passiveness does not stand a chance against proactivity.

I have found out that luck does not come for free

'Passiveness' a.k.a. 'waiting for things for happen' has never worked with me – great things have happened only because I have worked persistently for them. It is a word that does not exist in my vocabulary. ~~Passiveness~~ is what *might* work with some people, if they are extremely lucky. However, even if it does, it will be a one-time, temporary win. Do not leave things to chance. Luck comes to those, who work.

I have learned that patience and proactivity are always rewarded

Good old patience, coupled with proactivity, is a quality you have to develop so that you do not get discouraged if there are no immediate results, and will help you stay 'on top of things' – and in control of your life. Being patient is something that I still find hard to develop, but I am also learning how to take it easy, and reduce the pace a bit.

Lesson 3. Find a problem you care about and start solving it

One of the issues I am passionate about is gender equality for education, pay and job opportunities. While I was searching for the right career path in Denmark before my Master's graduation from Aarhus University, I had read many articles regarding gender inequality in the professional setting. I had heard countless discouraging rumors that it is harder to succeed as a woman in the tough business world. Of course, the scope is global, with challenges varying greatly from country to country, with the Nordics though being considered among the highest gender equality regions in the world.

When I was younger, between about ten-twelve, I always hoped that this 'gender inequality' thing people talked about was like a ghost – everyone discussed it, but no one had seen it. Strange how, in my early teenage years, I had never thought there was such a thing as 'gender inequality'; the twelve-year-old me, naïve and innocent, always believed in equal opportunity, regardless of gender, nationality or race, where the only decisive factors of success were ambition, drive, talent, knowledge, consistent work and motivation. Why should I be discriminated for a job opportunity (or salary), just because of my gender? It did not make any sense, it still does not. Regrettably, we can all only conclude that inequality and prejudices are not myths.

In Denmark, according to a joint analysis of the Danish Confederation of Trade Unions and the Danish Employers' Confederation, the wages of men are about 15 % higher than the wages of women – the benchmark being the same seniority of positions. Sad to say, this is still a good result, though, compared to the rest of the world. During the past years, Denmark has ranked among the top countries on gender equality in the Global Gender Gap Reports by the World Economic Forum.

On the other hand, it had always annoyed me deeply to hear prejudices about boys training ballet or dancesport, sports apparently perceived by many as "too feminine". At the same time, some girls are judged for doing "masculine" sports such as handball. This is a discrimination, regardless how you look at it.

There we come to another problem I care about – discrimination based on nationality. I found out that many international students worldwide had experienced 'discrimination' and prejudices against them, because of their country of origin. How ridiculous is that, indeed, some people judge others not based on character, motivation, skills and personality, but based on narrow-minded stereotypes.

The chances are, however, that if we all keep closing our eyes and saying the *'what can we do'* speech, nothing will ever change. Now that would be scary.

There are many genuine reasons to why we should focus our energy on working towards what feels valuable and meaningful to us, and struggle to make this difference, not for ourselves, but for others, who have even bigger burden of who-knows-what discrimination in the way. I admit that worrying about it, and being angry at the unfairness, which I could not influence, was a concern and an expenditure of energy that could not bring any value to the lives of many. However, when I spot unfairness, I always search for a way to eliminate it.

Therefore, I could not keep this unfairness locked in a box, because it is a burden for many people. We are not as powerless against such problems as we may think, even though sometimes I feel exhausted at fighting against injustice.

Therefore, I do not believe that we should ignore problems that are outside of our 'direct' control, or close our eyes to any sort of discrimination. Quite the opposite. Imagine, given that there is still gender inequality that puts a glass ceiling[19] on the professional development of women in Europe, where the countries value gender equality, what it is like in the developing markets in the world.

If you are discriminated against based on gender, nationality or ethnical background, remember that it is not your fault. It is the result of poor judgment of those who are led by such prejudices. It has nothing to do with your worth, and has everything to do with their stereotypes.

The above is an example of a topic I am passionate about – or specifically, passionate *against* –discrimination based on gender and nationality. What is it that you care about? Apparently, the world we

---

[19] Transparent barrier, by means of an unfair system that prevents people from achieving what they most deserve.

live in is full of problems and issues, and it needs us, proactive and never-resting people, to solve them.

Wrap-up

As the last two chapters cover many aspects of pursuing international career, I would like to structure everything mentioned as clearly as possible. Therefore, here is a summary of the main lessons shared:

1. **Patience and persistence win over passiveness.** Do not wish for luck – wish for courage, efficiency and the ability to work towards your goals. Never wait for things to happen to you, but pluck up the courage to work towards them.

2. **Do not lose touch with what you love doing**. I have learned that there is no such thing as 'not the right time' to follow your dreams. What is it that you've always wanted to do or create? You can bring a great idea and solution to life, if you have the passion for it.

3. **Stand out**. Present your background in a way that shows **your real personality.** Do not be anxious about being different and thinking outside of the box. Do not be too humble in terms of your achievements, efforts and strengths.

4. **Know your development needs.** Nevertheless, be honest about your weaknesses. Admit your limitations, and find a way to improve them (see Chapter 6).

5. **Don't stop learning.** There is no such thing as being 'accomplished enough'. Everything you learn is only a foundation for you to continue developing. Turn mistakes into your pool of lessons learned. Be open for opportunities. I am still figuring out what I would like to do – every day.

6. **Hold on to your principles**. I get extremely unnerved by things that do not feel right, and always speak up openly when something is out of place. You must be true to yourself, clichéd as it is, and not do what you think people would approve of; instead stand up for what is right, do not compromise your ethics, and go after what you want, and what makes you happy.

7. **Find an issue you care about**. Admit what is meaningful to you, and where you would like to make a difference, and then start solving the problem. You may think, *'Who am I to change the world? It is much bigger than me'*, and this is where you are wrong. If not you, then who?

8. **The fact that you are a good person does not mean automatically that great things will happen right away.** What to do? Be the person that makes you proud, stand up for integrity and keep striving to make a difference.

9. **Hiring only local talent no longer works in a globalized world.** Fact.

10. **Have confidence in your ideas and act upon them.** If you have an exciting idea you believe will bring a positive change in your life or contribute to the wellbeing of others, go for it. Alternatively, the more you work towards your vision, the more passionate you will become about your goals, despite the struggles you may encounter. This is so because Passion and Action proceed and follow each other. You decide which you start with first.

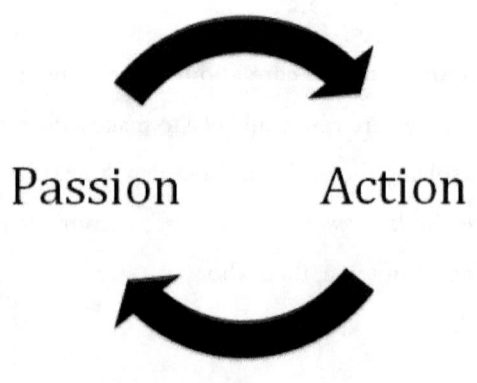

11. **Find the place you want to be in in the world.** Aspire to travel and to try new things and experiences – they shape your viewpoints, and help you find where you would like to be – not only geographically, but also career-wise.

12. **Write down your goals.** Last, but not least, put on paper your aspirations. This enhances your mental accountability, and pushes you to take actions.

Epilogue

All goals are realistically achievable, even if you are on your own in a 'country far, far away'. What I also found out was that 'staying quiet' about unfairness is not going to make it disappear, and I want to make a change for you. Because I care. I believe in integrity, honesty and fairness; I always have, and I want to believe that many of you do as well, regardless of the difficulties and unfairness you have faced in life. And our big, wonderful, but very much messed-up world needs people like us, who want to change it. Raise your voice, and if your talent is not 'spotted', do not sit back and wait; instead admit what feels valuable to you, make choices, plan, be prepared to expend a great amount of patience, and go make your dreams come true.

To sum up again, from my international experience, I have found out and strongly believe that there are six P's that drive the awesome life and the international career you deserve, namely: **Patience, Persistence, Passion, (Dreams) Plan, Purpose,** and **Proactivity**.

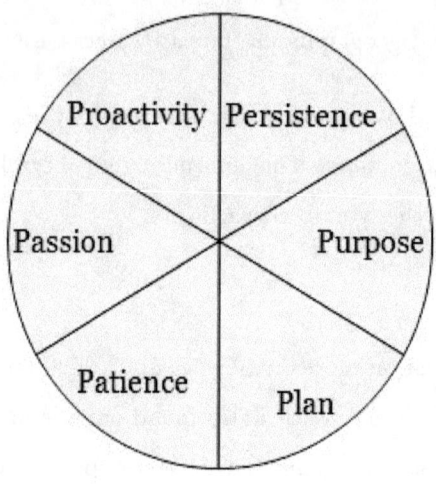

PART THREE: THE SHAPE OF THE MULTINATIONAL LIFE

Choices and Reflections

Chapter Nine – Finding the Right Place

Copenhagen

Pursuing an international education was why I moved abroad and what got me 'out there' in a foreign country, at only eighteen years of age. I wanted the world to be my working place, with no borders as to what I could be and what I could achieve. Finding my 'Dream City', on the other hand, was the main factor that, five years later when I was free to choose, to leave, affected my decision to stay in my second homeland.

I like to believe that every one of us has found, or will find at some point in their lives, a place which they call home, where they feel they belong and where they are always dragged back to. This place feels special, but not in a hometown kind of way. Hometown brings feelings of warmth, bond, familiarity, safety, and comfort. The place that I describe creates overwhelming feelings of excitement, belonging and anticipation. I have heard many stories of people feeling in the right place in New York City, but I also have many friends who feel the same way for other places around our planet, which also explains why my friends are spread around the world. I have visited many cities and beautiful capitals that have made a great impression on me, but I never felt this special attachment to any of them – until I stepped into Wonderful Copenhagen for the first time, in 2011.

Every city has a distinctive personality, a character of its own. Copenhagen is driven, yet composed, laid-back, yet dynamic, considerate but provocative. I knew right away that this was the city where I wanted to live. I had never experienced such a strong feeling of being 'in the right place' in my life, which was inexplicable and odd, and probably a bit insane, but was also extremely special and real. I never wanted to let this feeling go.

Aarhus was my home for five years. It was the perfect city for my university years – dynamic, cozy, and full of life, and I was thankful for all it had given me during the years of my education. However, I never felt an attachment or desperate desire to live in Aarhus after I was done with university. This was probably also because, after graduation, my friends and classmates spread out around Europe (and the world). I knew that I would always have my sentimental feelings for the great time I had in Aarhus, for the people I have met, and for the park of Aarhus University, with its magnificent surroundings, the lake and green fields, and the glass building of the AULA that reflected the sun's rays. No doubt, Aarhus had been ranked the best student city in the world. And it had left a mark. Most importantly, however, I felt like I had already left my mark there too and it was time to move on. I recognized the feeling immediately – as I had felt the same way about my hometown Burgas, after my high school graduation; when I knew I had to try something else.

Have you ever experienced a flashback when setting foot in a new place, as if you have lived there before? That was how I felt the first time I was in the Danish capital. The streets, the sea, the wonderful lakes, and the colourful buildings of inner Copenhagen made me fall in love in an instant. One of the memories that come to my mind of my first days there, was the time I got up in the Round Tower (Rundetårn), located in central Copenhagen, which was built as an astronomic observatory in 1642. The top floor, representing a round, open balcony, gave a generous panoramic view of the city. You could not exactly spot The Little Mermaid from there, but the view of the cathedrals rising in the sky, the residence of the Royal family – Amalienborg Palace, then further ahead – the offshore wind turbines in the distance, and the red brick rooftops of the picturesque buildings, was one of the most amazing (city) sights I have seen. Believe it or not, even the sight from the 84 floor of the Empire State Building could not beat that for me.

How to Thrive Abroad

The vibes of the city and the fairy-tale-like architecture of Greater Copenhagen left a mark as no other city or place had before. Every time I was walking by the Copenhagen lakes, and later enjoying the soft, gold sunset over the harbour at Islands Brygge, I wished the time could freeze. The only time I had felt this way had been when visiting my family in Burgas. Sometimes we had so few days to be together, I wished the time could stop for us.

We all know that, most often, it is not about the place but the people you are with that makes us feel at peace. However, I hardly knew anyone in Copenhagen back then, but I felt love-struck. Well, it still was not Burgas. Nowhere really was. My hometown was remarkable, unique, incomparable. However, Copenhagen got me by surprise, creating in me all these new feelings with the beauty of its own.

I loved the immediate feeling of belonging. The first time I was in the Danish capital, the sunshine was bathing the whole city, and the lakes resembled ocean made of crystals, uplighting everything in silver. I could not take my eyes of the sight. The bridges, the swans, the buildings overlooking the sea, the sun-path reflected over it, sometimes replaced by the reflection of the clouds, the coast and the willow trees: everything looked as if it were taken out of a fairy tale. Except that it was real and I was part of it.

I remember I was walking down the main shopping street Strøget; I was fascinated by the mixture of liveliness, energy and harmony. The shops, the cozy cafes, the City Hall Square and the fountains looked magnificent! Full of life, yet everyone seemed very relaxed. People looked as if they were actually enjoying being there, instead of rushing to somewhere else. Thinking of the main streets and squares in Moscow, London, New York, Berlin, Mumbai and all the other big cities or capitals I had been to, I could not find a comparison with this mixture of easy-goingness and energetic lifestyle. It was a captivating blend of nature, dynamics and harmony.

Jasen had always wondered 'what was wrong' while we were sitting in the train on our way back to Aarhus, at the time when I was still studying at AU (*'You always seem so sad when we are leaving Copenhagen; it is like a shadow comes over your face'*). Ah, my dear emotions, always there, written all over my face.

'I feel like I am leaving home, instead of 'going home' right now, if it makes sense at all,' I used to say, staring out of the window at the disappearing brick buildings as the train pulled us away from Copenhagen Central Station.

Jasen joked that I had post-Copenhagen blues; in fact, I think he was right. Was that how so many people felt about New York City? I was tired of feeling nostalgic every time I left the city; it just did not feel right. Besides, I lived in beautiful Aarhus, where my friends, my boyfriend, my job and university were, while my family was living in my sweet hometown Burgas. Ironically, I felt 'homesick' in every other (gorgeous) city, small town and capital I had visited, regardless of how fantastic a time I was having there. This covered most of the other Danish cities, as well as a short period of living in fairy-tale Moscow, then New York, spending one week in fascinating Mumbai, and visiting old and stunning European cities such as Sofia, Budapest, Paris, Rome, London, Gothenburg, Vienna, Florence, amongst others. All of them were beautiful in their unique way. But I had never felt *like staying*.

However, my pride in my flawless sense of orientation disappeared the second day I had officially moved to live in Copenhagen. I went out to do a tour around the city by myself – it was my first time and 'date' alone with Copenhagen, and I could not wait to explore it. I arrived at Kongens Nytorv square by metro, planning to head to Christiansborg Slot, which is the Danish Parliament Palace in central Copenhagen, and then enjoying the day by the canal next to the Royal Library.

Even though I had been to the city some times before, I couldn't remember which way the Parliament was, and on top of this, I couldn't use online navigation as my mobile was out of battery. Hence, I looked around like a confused tourist, and I thought, *'This is just unfair… If only I had a map, I would have found the palace already.'* At that very moment an

Asian woman, as confused as me, came over with a map and asked me: '*Excuse me, can you show me how to reach Christiansborg Palace?*'

A very popular place indeed. I took over her colourful map with the confidence of the local that I was not. After struggling to find which 'gade' we were at, and where the short-cut road was, my patience ran out and I stopped a very polite and helpful local girl, who showed us the shortest way. How embarrassing. A month later, though, I could walk everywhere in the central city of Copenhagen with my eyes closed.

Even now, years later, very time I am wandering in the Royal Garden (Kongens Have) towards the Rosenborg Palace – one of my favourite places in the world – I feel unconditional happiness and peacefulness, for no obvious reason, but just because I can be there. During the spring, the garden leading to the castle is a magnificent sight, colored in deep sky-blue from the violet tulips. My friends and I enjoy spending time there especially during the summer days, when the sun and rain have fed the greenness.

Speaking of summer, nothing compares to Copenhagen during the warm days. I have my top favourite spots, but there are so many more historic landmarks and unique sights. When the long Nordic summer days arrive, my friends know where to find me after working hours – reading a book and drinking *iskaffe* in Kongens Have, sitting next to the water at Islands Brygge, sunbathing at the Black Diamond or having a glass of wine outside Ofelia Plads or at the Royal Danish Opera in Holmen.

There are places where, without clear logical reason, you feel at home. Pure emotional and spiritual joy! I was stunned by everything about one city: its sunrises and sunsets, the bright blue sky, the rain and snow, wind and freezing temperature, the long winter – I wanted all of it – as long as it was in Copenhagen. This was how I realized that I would be a global citizen for life.

Epilogue

I have moved to live in Copenhagen in January 2015, only three months after my graduation from university, for starting a job there. When I settled in the Danish capital, I could hardly believe I was going to be a resident in the city, not just a tourist until sunset. It sounds crazy but it felt like being reunited with the love of my life, after a lifetime (even though the actual love of my life stayed in Aarhus for another year, to finalize his studies).

Rationality is important when deciding where to live and settle. Safety, work opportunities within your areas of expertise, being with your significant other, living not far distance from an airport, and many more factors are of course decisive. However, I had found out that logic is not enough. You should allow yourself to add *gut feeling*, to discover the place where you really want to live: the place where 'it feels right'. Reflect on what you feel when you are in an incredibly beautiful and prosperous place, but it seems distant and you are not at peace. When it feels like it is not enough, and you are daydreaming about being somewhere else.

After all, love is irrational too. I bet you have probably experienced the following: there is this amazing person, with a great personality, who is caring, thoughtful, smart, funny, handsome, treats you well, and is very attracted to you. But you are not attracted to them at all. I know I have experienced these situations, and I have wished I felt something for that person, but I could not and never did. It should come as no surprise that you cannot really 'force' a feeling, if there is no chemistry and affection. Apparently, the same is valid when choosing the place to live. Rationality and feelings – it is not one versus the other, but instead the combination of both that makes the best possible choice. As a person who usually makes decisions based on facts and logic, it is a paradox to conclude that, from my expatriate journey, I have learned that often we do not need a 'real', logical reason to stay, nor to leave. Sometimes it just *has to feel right*, and that is more than enough. I learned that home is a feeling.

Chapter Ten – Ten Things I Wish I had Known Before I Moved Abroad

Expectations and Anticipation

Before I left my home country to pursue a higher education in Denmark back in 2009, I had extensively researched as much as possible about not only my future-to-be university but also naturally the country I was to live in. I had read articles, tourist guides, encyclopedias, and had also been reaching out to students who were already living in Aarhus. Hence, I had received much good advice about life in Denmark, student unions and practicalities that I believed were essential to know about, such as accommodation availability, student job opportunities, prices, and more.

I knew the student housing application website, I knew how to reach the university campus (by bus, bike, or on foot), I found out the country had the maximum temperature of 22-25 Celsius during the summer (which was ideal for me), that Denmark had a good social system, and that in general people spoke fluent English. My knowledge about Denmark went on to include the writer Hans Christian Andersen, the discovery that Denmark had some of the most delicious *kager* in the world, and that the country had a solid focus on

The Shape of the Multinational Life

sustainability and green energy. The locals also seemed to be extremely fond of biking as a main type of transportation.

I had also found out that my favourite athletes and dancesport couple in the world was a Bulgarian-Danish dream team who resided and trained in Denmark (I was also lucky enough to meet them just two months after arriving). I knew I was going to live in a city called Aarhus[20] and that it was, as it seemed from all the pictures that popped up on Google, delightful.

However, as it turned out, this was not nearly enough when it came to what I needed to know during my first weeks in the country. Of course, finding out as much as possible about the environment of my new homeland was worth it; thanks to my research I knew a bit about what to expect.

While I was still within the borders of safety back home, I never thought of or expected all the frustration, unforeseen challenges, culture shock, cultural differences and the dilemmas I was about to face. Back home, I was convinced that everything else was probably

---

[20] Aarhus University had some of its English-taught business undergraduate programmes taught in Herning – a small Danish town on the Western part of Jutland, approximately 130 km away from Aarhus. You can imagine the surprise to some international students, to discover (post-arrival) that their campus was situated in another town. Another proof of why being as well prepared as possible is better than leaving things to chance. Even if you like surprises.

common sense. All I had was an idea what it was to pursue an international education and career abroad, and a rather unclear mental picture of what it would be like.

On the other hand, I never wished I had known 'it all', as this would have made many experiences less fun and exciting. Anticipation is a gift too! You cannot be 100% prepared for everything, unless you experience it yourself. You will learn and find out the important things along the way. What you could do in advance, however, is to be as well prepared as possible, to ensure a smooth life transition. The best way to do it is to hear firsthand experience and advice from someone who 'has been there'.

Therefore, I have prepared a list of the top ten things I realize now *I wish I'd known* before I moved to live in Denmark. Some are much more important than others, and they are applicable and relatable to many other countries in the world. As the previous chapters have covered most of the aspects in details, the following list is a concise overview of the top things to be aware of when moving to live abroad.

I wish I'd known:

1. TO LEAVE STEREOTYPES BEHIND

Danes are *not* culturally the same as the Brits and the Americans. The fact that the countries are 'Western' does not mean they are culturally similar, my dear, naïve, eighteen-year-old me.

My initial expectations were significantly different from the reality. I blame my cultural unawareness to the fact that I had probably watched so many American TV shows and movies (*One Tree Hill, Breaker High, Gilmore Girls*), which had formed the idea in my head that all Western countries have the same or similar behaviour. Not exactly.

My Danish friends are some of the most outgoing and outspoken people that I know. However, it took me time to understand them, and when I first arrived in Denmark I thought too local people were reserved. Coming from a South-East European country like Bulgaria, where people are outspoken and no one is afraid to show their feelings or to involve you in conversations, I had never experienced the opposite. I noticed the difference during my first days in the country, where all I was meeting were shy glances and I couldn't help, but thinking, *'is there something wrong with me in Denmark?'*

According to my friends from Denmark, Danes try not to invade your privacy, which is why many foreigners initially may perceive them as 'reserved'. Apparently, it is because people are trying to mind their own business. Every time someone asks me whether Danes are 'cold', I think of all my amazing, warm and outgoing Danish friends and colleagues, and I fight the urge to start laughing. That would be the last word I would use to describe them. Regardless, I agree that probably people tend to be a bit reserved at first, and perhaps seem somehow shy. The cheerful, emotional and over-excited me has been asked in Denmark occasionally whether I was drunk. I was not. It was just my temperamental personality, people, I had moods, feelings and emotions. Yet, my inner voice still reminds me often: *stop smiling at strangers, stop smiling at strangers.*

As a newcomer, Danes may have appeared reserved, but that is because they have a high respect for privacy and are sometimes afraid not to be 'embarrassed' by their English-language skills (despite being fluent!). After I found out about my misjudgment, I got used to the new reality, but it took one hell of a year to feel really integrated. Once you know such culturally embedded differences, life abroad gets much easier.

One of the best lessons I have learned was that nationality/country of origin does not define a person. Full stop. I have learned that there is no culture that could be perceived as 'too similar'. Hofstede and Ghemawat's research have suggested some useful frameworks for comparing cultures and countries within different parameters and dimensions, as I have previously mentioned throughout the book, which can partly explain in theory cultural behaviour in a society. However, can such research actually define us? I read the dimensions for Bulgaria, and I hardly fit anywhere. Cultural awareness is best learned by experience. Nevertheless, you should have an open mind! I cannot emphasize this enough. Cultural awareness is highly important, but assuming similarities can lead to surprise and disappointment. People are different! Be open-minded, don't pass judgment too fast, and leave stereotypes and prejudices behind you.

2. ABOUT LEARNING THE LOCAL LANGUAGE

Living abroad and speaking a foreign language every day is difficult, and fluency is a long process that hardly ends. This is the truth, plain, evident and simple.

When I moved to Denmark, I could not help, but feeling jealous of my friends from Germany or the Nordic countries, or those who had studied German language beforehand. They seemed to grasp the Danish language so much faster. I'd studied Russian in High School, and I am native Bulgarian, so despite my fluency in English, I had my Scandinavian language challenges. If I'd known it was going to be that hard, I would probably have found time and started learning Danish already in Bulgaria; or do anything that would have helped me learn the local language faster. I must add that I do not regret for a second learning Russian, but I think sometimes that some extra proficiency skills would have been valuable too. Do not underestimate the local language proficiency, even if you live in a country such as Denmark, where everyone is flawless in English. Your social life will be richer and your integration – easier.

3. ABOUT THE STUDENT ACCOMMODATION

The dormitories (i.e. the student housing) require a deposit, which equals three times the rent, aside from the first month rent itself. I wish I'd known that this did not mean *'pre-paying three rents in advance'* and that I still had to pay the next three months anyway. And thus, be prepared to have savings, regardless of the 'three rents' deposit. Am I the only one who had misunderstood their student housing rules? The student houses in Denmark have great conditions, and most of them are fully furnished, so at least that compensates for the more expensive rent and deposit. Moreover, with an hourly student job you can be financially independent.

When it comes to having your deposit refunded after moving out, personally I have changed many apartments for the past eight years – ten to be exact, and have never had an issue having this refunded.

However, regardless of where you are, be aware of the terms and conditions around the deposit.

4. ABOUT CULTURE SHOCK

Culture shock, sudden and unexpected nostalgia, and the frustration with the fast-paced lifestyle arrived faster than anticipated, and were inevitable. I wish someone had hinted to me about all that mess; I wish I had received any advice, to be somehow better prepared.

Although such advice would not have prevented my experience with culture shock, at least it would have set some expectations; reminding me that it was normal and I was not the only one.

5. THAT LONG-DISTANCE RELATIONSHIPS ARE POSSIBLE...

If you both desire to be part of each other lives. Long-distance relationships can endure, even the furthest distance for the longest time. But only in the case that both people want it, commit to it, and really desire to be with each other.

I wished someone had told me that it was worth working hard for it. Because I found out that once you finally get to be together, the experience is just indispensable; nothing can compare to it. It makes the relationship – and every moment spent together – the most precious thing in the world. It does require effort, and a lot of patience, as well as a huge dose of Skype, and compromises. In the end, it also demands common planning, regarding the future living situation.

It is not easy, it is worse than they present it in the movies, but it makes your relationship incredibly strong, as well as your love. I found out that there is no better way to test a relationship than enduring a long-distance period (Chapter 11).

6. ABOUT AFTER-GRADUATION CAREER DILEMMAS, AND WHAT IT TAKES

Pursuing an international career depends a lot on your patience and persistence, drive as well as networking. All of that, apart from relevant experience, good grades, talent, language skills, integrity you have. Landing your dream job abroad is about doing what you can within your control, in order to make things happen. Proactivity pays off and always wins (Chapter 7 and 8).

7. ABOUT THE SLOW PACE OF INTEGRATION

My favourite brands (well, my favourite brands prior to my time in Denmark) could not be found in Denmark. They simply did not exist there (and I am not even speaking about Bulgarian brands, but about international ones). I appreciate the protectionism of the local economy, of course, and I know this is common sense, but you should be aware that, despite the globalization, you will be surprised to find how many 'global' brands that you are familiar with and are found everywhere in your home country are not available abroad. I remember how I asked my Danish neighbors during my first week in Aarhus about where exactly I could find a particular favourite chewing gum brand. My neighbors looked at each other, confused, and then turned to me and asked, '*Misha, what exactly is this? We have never heard of it before.*' Had I moved to Mars?

I was heartbroken. I might exaggerate, but I remember that even though I was a craving-for-exploring-new-things foreigner, in my heart, that of a recently arrived international student, I was missing everything 'home-like'.

As time passes, you will not crave your old favourite brands as strongly. You will even start missing the 'local' brands when you travel abroad or go 'home' again (Chapter 5). Until then, maybe fill your luggage with your favourite products, or order online where possible. During my first year in Denmark, my parents and my friends, concerned for my well-being (and convinced that I would not survive otherwise), used to send me treats (and warm clothes, despite how many times I had explained to my friends they were selling such in

Aarhus too) from back home. The gesture itself was enough to warm me deeply, but I had realized also that this had made my first months abroad bearable.

Moreover, as a books addict, I must add the bookstores in Denmark sell books primarily in Danish and English. This was another surprise for me, because in Bulgaria I was used to being able to find a wide variety of books, including classics and new writing, in English, Russian, German, French, Spanish and many other languages. This is not the case everywhere, but it does encourage you to practise the local language.

8. ABOUT THE LOCAL WEATHER CONDITIONS

Not to undermine the 'umbrella' business, but to me it seems almost useless to buy one in Denmark (honestly), even though it looks like it rains every second day. Dear eighteen-year-old me, you should have invested in several rain jackets. Most of the time, the rain is accompanied by strong wind, which makes it useless to use umbrellas. If you are going to live in Denmark or Scandinavia, go and buy a rain jacket instead, especially if you are considering biking daily (which you probably would). Before I came to Denmark, I had heard rumors about the Danish 'breeze'. Whoever decided to call the sharp, cold, restless Danish wind a 'breeze' owes me about nine umbrellas. There is no winning against the Danish wind.

On a more serious note, few of my classmates from my Bachelor's dropped out during the first semester, because they thought they could not endure the weather conditions. If you dream about tropical climate and heat, Scandinavia would perhaps not be the best place for you to live. Personally, I do not mind the local weather; in fact, the spring and summer days in Denmark are as fantastic as they can be. The winters are dark and cold, true. But so are they in Bulgaria and most of Europe.

9. HOW TO MOVE FROM SURVIVAL TO WINNING MODE

I wished I had known from the start that regardless of how driven and proactive a person is, he or she can always get stuck in a 'mode of survival' when first moving abroad. No matter how well prepared you are, you will face adversity, and this can lead to shifting your life focus to seek comfort and safety instead of progress, achieving goals and development.

Nevertheless, I found out that feeling safe and holding your ground is the prerequisite for striving to succeed, thrive and develop.

The important lesson is not to stay too long in the comfort zone, but to pluck up the courage to go after what you want, by not focusing on your limitations as a foreigner but instead on your strengths and advantages, with a strong can-do spirit. I wished I knew that all obstacles were my path to being mature and resilient. When I look back now at least, I see that clearly.

Perceive the challenges and obstacles as a way to move forward, to improve and develop, not as a reason to hide behind safety chains. Get over the survival mode by having a clear vision, plan and process of development, and always remember to help others too.

10. ABOUT THE CLASH OF WORLDS AND THAT NOTHING IS AS IMPOSSIBLE AS IT SEEMS

It takes time to feel at home in a foreign country, but eventually it happens. I really wish my twenty-five-year-old self could have appeared magically six years ago and had a good encouraging talk with my freshly-arrived-in-Denmark self. I wish the experienced me could tell the eighteen-year-old Mihaela the fact that it would take some time, but that one day I would feel at home in Denmark, too. I wish I could tell her that she would be completely in love with the small fairy-tale-like Nordic country, with its amazing castles, beautiful sea surroundings, freezing winters and often freezing summers, and the Wonderful Copenhagen. That she would miss it all madly when travelling to other countries, and would crave its local dishes, treats and even the inconsistent weather. Something that seemed impossible years ago.

But I also know that I have managed to feel at peace with myself, and have a strong sense of belonging, have a vision and work for it with consistence. If only I knew at the beginning how I would feel in just some years, this would have saved me so much frustration and heartache.

Not to succeed, or not get what you want, even after all the efforts, is not bad, but never trying is tragic. When I look back at the last six-seven years spent abroad, I do not measure achievements by the one-sided *success versus failure* formula. Instead, I think of all the tough situations, when all I wanted to do was hide under the blankets or pack my luggage and leave, but instead I had chosen to come out, and welcome life-changing decisions.

Epilogue

Encountering huge doses of uncertainty and challenges abroad is inevitable. When you move to live abroad, there is only so much you can do, research and learn about the new culture and the local-specific differences.

Save yourself the unnecessary stress of unfulfilled expectations by being open-minded(-hearted) enough to learn and explore the new culture, its traditions and society norms; then the journey turns into adventure.

It is thrilling to learn the rest by means of your own experience. However, knowing what to expect can save you a lot of frustration. Read books and talk to other foreigners living there, by means of forums, social media groups and blogs, or by asking a friend of a friend in your network. We are now as connected as never before. When consulting about the new country, make sure you take into consideration a broader sample size of expatriates. Even though people experience the same phenomenon (read 'culture'), you will see that they significantly differ in their *perspectives*. Therefore, always make sure to hear more than one opinion about the expatriate life and integration in a country. Do that for the sake of building a well-rounded perspective. Then be open-minded to form your own judgment by personal experience and your individually gained insights.

Chapter Eleven – The Sky Over Home

Living Between Places

As an expatriate, you live in a constantly changing environment, requiring continuous adaptation, and this can sometimes result in burnout. I have learned that the only way to deal with these emotions is to change your viewpoint. Living abroad indeed brings many challenges, but it also carries an exciting and amazing experience, as well as an exclusive opportunity to learn and develop personally and professionally to the best possible extent.

During my first two years spent abroad, regardless of how good life was to me, 'missing' had become an inevitable part of my life as an expatriate – always, and every day. Even though I did not feel it consciously, I knew it was somewhere there, at the back of my mind. During my first year in Denmark, I was missing my family and friends from Bulgaria terribly. While I was in Bulgaria, I then missed my life and friends in Denmark to an enormous extent. Regardless of where I was, my mind was never completely at peace. Back then, my perspective led to such frustration that I even thought I could never be happy.

Hence, instead, what I *chose* to feel and believe was that *I could have it all* – the best from my both worlds. I convinced myself that I was very lucky, and was thankful for and extremely happy with the life I chose. The new perspective gradually transformed my international life from 'chaos and frustration' to harmony, but it did not happen without effort and daily reminders of the positive side of the story. I had two places called home. I also found out that you can either believe that you belong *nowhere*, or that you belong *everywhere*.

You should never place conditions on happiness. You have probably heard many times how 'happiness is found within us' and that it is a matter of mindset and perspective – I have always thought that was just a cheesy cliché, but there is a lot of truth in it. Happiness depends mainly on how resilient we are and how we perceive and respond to our circumstances.

I have found out that happiness is achieved by changing your attitude and by being grateful for everything good in your international life, instead of focusing on what is missing in it. It is indeed a state of mind, before it is a state of heart.

What you cannot prevent, however, is the reappearing nostalgia, and waves of sudden sadness. It hits you when you least expect it, often without warning or a specific reason. Can you ever get over it? Probably someday, and from my experience its amount and frequency of occurrence gradually decreases over time, but you can never get rid of nostalgia entirely. Speaking of mindset, instead of letting yourself feel sad and miserable over 'missing' something, perceive this feeling as an indicator that there is another place out there, where you have people who you love: a place where you also belong, where you feel at home. You are truly lucky and blessed to have such.

After almost seven years of living abroad, I have still caught myself wondering what the sky over Bulgaria, the sky over my mum and dad, looked like at that very moment, while I stared at the 'Danish' sky, with its rain clouds or its sun shining brightly over the city. I have daydreamed like that, out of the blue, even when being with friends at AROS[21] rainbow, or looking out of Rundetaarn's roof, staring out of my window at home, or while commuting by S-train. Has the sun set in Burgas already? Is the sky so bright and clear? What forms do the clouds have at that moment there?

Nostalgia loves to come around also when I travel abroad – no matter where in the world. It usually arrives only several days into my stay, and this time it hits the place in my heart where Denmark is. I'm slightly embarrassed to admit it, but as much as I love traveling, I am often longing for going back to Copenhagen, after staying somewhere abroad for longer than a week. My phone's weather app is always scheduled to Copenhagen, no matter where I am, because it gives me

---

[21] Modern Arts Museum located in Aarhus, where the top floor is a round colourful terrace, offering a panoramic view of Aarhus.

the relief and reassurance of knowing what is going on back home, where my life is. Even if the forecast is for a grey, depressing rainy sky, it always cheers me up, and I am looking forward to get back there under the dark sky, wet to the bones.

I was asked by my friends on New Year's Eve in 2017 whether I think Denmark has changed a lot during the past years, since I had moved there in 2009. What I knew for sure was that Denmark has changed a lot in my perspective, and in the way I felt about living in the country. My life there means so much to me now. However, 'Denmark' was a big question mark for me several years ago. Before I came to study there, it was 'just' the Scandinavian country of endless green fields, home of Hans Christian Andersen's Little Mermaid. It was the small Nordic country 'only a span away' from Bulgaria, according to my world map on the wall. It was the place where my top choice of university was located.

For the past seven years, Denmark has turned to be the country of the fascinating wind turbine parks, LEGO, my Aarhus University ALUMNI network, the witty Christmas nisse,[22] my dream career, the

---

[22] Danish Christmas (mischievous) elves – mythological creatures from the Scandinavian folklore, and an inevitable part of Danish Christmas traditions, legends and decorations.

UN Youth Association team of goodwill ambassadors that I am part of, and the love of my life.

Denmark has also become the country where I feel in the right place, despite not being the country I was born in. Since my friends are spread all over Europe now, it would be fair to say that Denmark is also the country hosting *some* of my close friends. In other words, the small Nordic country has turned out to be my home. However, it did not take only logical and rational thinking in making up my mind whether Denmark would remain my 'home'. In theory, if my choice was purely based on rationality, there is a big chance I would have left Denmark after graduation. The best choices I have done are a result of a mixture of gut-feelings and solid facts. What do I mean by this? I am sure you have heard the expression 'I knew in my guts', when you cannot necessarily explain something rationally but you sense that it is right (or wrong). Even though I consider myself a 'logic and facts' person, the best choices I have made, ironically, are when I've let my senses decide. Trust the facts, but follow your instincts.

Facts and Feelings. Illustration by C'MNKY Art

I am often told that *I like to chase the wind.* This means that I am constantly in search of a special and unique state of mind and soul – the gut (and chest) feeling that says I am in the right place. As a result, I have been often told that I am going after illusions and idealism. Probably. But wasn't I chasing the wind as well, when I had decided to pursue my higher education in Denmark? I had an idea in my head of what I would like to achieve, but I could never have known for sure what it was going to be, and whether I would manage to find what I was looking for. But I now know for sure that I did find it. I believe in taking risks.

Catching your breath and choosing a life of an international student or expatriate is like chasing the wind too. Leaving the comfort zone in pursuit of an idea or a dream, despite what everyone else says, is practically chasing the wind. It is the same as pursuing your ideal of love. You need high drive, determination and a strong *certainty* that you will find it.

Going after the wind, or so we are told, is against logic. However, would you rather live in a compromise and a big reserve of 'what ifs'? If that were the alternative, I would rather chase the unknown, if there was even a small chance that I may find *it* – the feeling of belonging, fulfilled goals and dreams, and the opportunity to experience new adventures, to learn and thrive.

Even though I felt like I had an accomplished life in Aarhus, and even though I was born and had lived in Burgas for eighteen years, I have never felt more in the right place as I have in Copenhagen. No doubt that Burgas and Aarhus are irreplaceable and special – forever, both for different reasons. My hometown Burgas for being the best learning and development place in the world, for which I will never be able to thank enough the people who literally built me – my amazing family, friends, teachers and coaches. Even when you travel the world, you still would not able to find a better place than the one where your parents are.

Aarhus, on the other hand, is special for showing me that dreams come true – sooner or later; for allowing me to meet the right people at the right time and place, and teaching me most of the lessons I am sharing with you in this book. However, my time in Aarhus should take the credit mostly for proving to me that it is possible to dust yourself off and make 'things' happen, despite all obstacles, difficulties and 'impossible' situations.

Once, I was sitting in the bus going back to Copenhagen, after spending a weekend in Aarhus, and my eyes came across a signboard on the road before we exited the city. The sign said 'Den Gamle By' (The Old City). I turned my head immediately to the right and gazed at the road leading down to the Old City with the hope that I may see something else. Because I knew what was only several metres down the road. It would lead you to the Botanical Gardens, which meant that only a heartbeat away was the business faculty of Aarhus University – Aarhus Business and Social Science, and the reason I had come to Denmark; the choice that had changed my life forever.

Yet every time the bus gets on the Storebælt to Zealand (known as The Great Belt Link)[23], I feel that I am on the right track, on the right path. I am also aware that this excitement and anticipation have

---

[23] The 254-metre-long bridge connecting the island of Sjælland (Zealand) with the island of Fyn.

nothing to do with the fact that the bus is travelling above the sea for approximately twenty minutes, nor are due to the astonishing horizon of nothing but shining water ahead. The overwhelming feeling of warmth is because my heart realizes where I am heading to. Home. To Copenhagen.

All of the goals that have been accomplished are a result of *chasing the wind*. They are the outcome of going after the unknown, the untested, and the result of refusing to make a compromise with what I wanted the most.

Drive!

Start your journey of accomplishing your goals with a passion for making things happen, by acknowledging the efforts and time that achieving them will take. Dive onto the road *untraveled* (by you); have a clear vision of where you want to be, without a guarantee of what it is going to be, but knowing exactly how you want to *feel*.

This is what it takes to pursue an international life. You become a child of crossroads – you are neither *here* nor *there*. Living between places. Accepting 'missing' as part of your life, being ready to explore opportunities – all the time – and having the courage to deal with difficulties, to give up the reassurance of clearly defined cultural identity, but after overcoming these – constantly learning.

Epilogue

When you live in any other place in the world that is not your homeland, nostalgia is sticking around, no matter how happy you are in your new home. It is somehow always there in the background, often being ignored or forgotten due to the busyness of the everyday life.

However, your feelings about your new home country will change over time and they will grow stronger, if you *allow* yourself to experience and embrace all the new things it ushers into your life. These are, among others, new places, new languages and cultures. If you are open to *meet* new people, you *ask* for advice, you *listen, read, dream, plan, act* and don't *give up* on your goals and *on what is important to you*. Change and adjustment are not only a matter of time and gained experience, but mainly also a matter of mindset and how you perceive them.

Still, as much as I am happy and satisfied with my life abroad, I am well aware that nothing can compare to my homeland Bulgaria. Travelling back to Denmark after visiting my family in Bulgaria during vacations, I am left love-struck. On my way to the airport, I stare out the car window trying to capture it all: the landscape of ancient mountains, blur of dark green forests, deep purple lavender fields, and the sky over home. I am reminded of everything that I usually forget I'm missing, while watching it all slipping away from me. Again. And there comes the inevitable pain. I hate saying goodbye to my family every time I need to leave my hometown – I am not sure I can ever get used to that. Every time I come back to Denmark, I also realize, however, how insanely I missed my life there and how much I love both places. I have found that there is no release from these mixed feelings.

Once an expatriate, you are an expatriate for life. Once you go *that* road, there is no coming back from it. Repatriation is possible in theory, but in your mindset, your perspectives and world-view, *verdenen* is not the same anymore – it has changed forever, and so have you. You start seeing the world as an endless field of opportunities, which you are dying to explore. In your mindset, the world becomes a place without barriers. You will be constantly longing for new adventures, thriving in multicultural environments, in complex, changing, dynamic, international living, with a thirst for more knowledge that cannot be satisfied.

Your international culture mix is unique

Your culture will not be defined clearly. It will be formed as a mix of everything you have experienced. Mine is an international, Danish-Bulgarian culture mix in its own. Each expatriate has his or her own one, built and modified by the people, cultures, places, experiences, customs, and everything encountered once embarked upon an international life. It is part of the 'international culture' – even though the term is not entirely accurate, since it is not a general culture that every expatriate experiences and adopts, but rather a unique and very individual one.

By looking around you, you can find the 'signs' of the culture mix even in the little things of your daily life. At this moment, taking a glance around my desk, I can see the leads clearly. My international culture mix is, for example, well represented in my pencil case – accidentally, every single one carries its own history, forming my 'once upon a life' in Denmark.

The closest to me is a bright blue pen, which I got from Jasen when we started dating, and as sentimental as I apparently am, I have kept it, even though it has long ago run out of ink. Right next to it stands a black pen with my company logo on it, then a blue marker left from the time I was working for a big global corporation during my Master's, and a white pen with the Aarhus University logo. There is also a simple but favourite pencil that I took from my parents' house when I was in Bulgaria last winter. Finally, there are some pens from my travels and two pencils, representing a boy and a girl, bought from the 'Flying Tiger' as a joke with a close friend of ours on a night out in the city.

The international culture is not that different from the pencil case – it is colourful and diverse, and compiles in bits and pieces your multinational life.

The life of a global citizen is like living between two worlds

My solace is the belief that every 'goodbye' is a 'see you later'. Nowadays, nothing is really further than a span (or a flight) away. Every time I enter my beautiful, teenage room at my parents' house in Burgas, I realize how much I have changed and grown, but part of me has yet remained the same. The part that strives for achieving the impossible with strong drive and self-reliance, and the part that unconditionally loves Bulgaria and always will, and wants to stay there and never leave again the safe and secure place of home. However, the other part of me craves desperately the challenge and excitement that my international life in Denmark brings, and drags me back – right there, on the road via the Storebælt.

With regards to my long-distance relationship – I found out that I was wrong.

I was wrong that the distance would make love weaker. That it would fade, as a result. In contrast, if that was even possible, we love each other even more now. I was right about something else, though – love was enough to keep us together, while thriving in different worlds.

Therefore, I chose to tell you 'a story' of a long-distance relationship that survived despite the distance. After his graduation from high school, Jasen started his Bachelor's at Aarhus University, followed by a Master's degree in Denmark. We lived together in Aarhus until my graduation, after which I moved to Copenhagen, because of a job offer. We spent yet another year living apart, travelling between Jutland and Zealand every weekend, until we moved in together – again, this time in Copenhagen.

We celebrate every day that we are together – since the day we decided that we could beat the odds against the long-distance, because we were crazy about each other.

To trust your instincts is the worst yet the best advice I can give you. Worst, as it tells you nothing by itself and placed out of context; yet the best, because in this context it tells you everything – what you would like to be and where, while not losing track of where you come from.

What does it take to pursue an international life, to live a life outside of comfort zones?

Experiencing life shifts and welcoming constant change.

Living a complex, dynamic, international life, often on the road.

The Shape of the Multinational Life

Learning to approach everything with wonder, curiosity, courageousness, discovery and thirst for new experiences.

Having a big heart and thinking about others even more — because you know what it is to be on your own.

Making the most of the opportunities given to you, without knowing what is going to happen next.

Beings self-reliant — learning to survive and thrive on your own in the world, being less dependent on others, yet being always able to help and support people in need.

Fighting a feeling that something is missing.

Being extremely culturally aware and open-minded.

Knowing that if something is both terrifying and amazing, then you should pursue it.

Taking risks, without having any guarantees for anything.

Putting your trust in people whom you do not know at all, hoping they will give you a chance.

Not letting any bruises of disappointments discourage you.

Being able to easily change direction, but sticking to principles at the same time.

Being too brave for your own good.

Craving travelling; learning to adapt to a fast-paced environment.

Working with people from all over the world, from diverse backgrounds and with a different experience from yours. Listening to their amazing stories. Learning from each other.

Seeing the world as a field of possibilities – and thus becoming very good at spotting the right opportunities.

Standing often at a crossroad with one foot placed on each path.

Having more than one place called home in the world. After all, I often remind myself, I am so lucky to have these two only less than a span away from each other.

I realize also that, despite everything mentioned above, in my soul I am still the eighteen-year-old girl, who believes the world consists of opportunities, not limitations.

What is next on my road as a global citizen? My burning ambition has made many exciting plans for my international career – and I am not planning for settling for less.

Some of my next dreams are:

To continue to be a mentor for students and other young professionals like me and help them achieve their goals and career aspirations – be it abroad or not.

To lead sustainable business development projects supporting growth, strategy and innovation globally.

To be a United Nations Goodwill Ambassador – to have the opportunity to make a big difference for Education, Anti-Discrimination, Gender Equality and Children Protection and Development.

To be an influencer and to use my constantly growing knowledge, experience and skills to be useful and contribute to as many people as possible.

To keep travelling the world.

To write and publish a bestselling book, which offers the sort of material that gives people goose bumps – in the overwhelming way – and inspires and motivates them to turn their dreams into reality. A book that solves a problem that matters – to me and many others.

I also have a secret (not anymore), crazy dream to star in movies, such as Star Wars (well, who doesn't?) or inspirational commercials and campaigns that bring more beauty to our world.

I also dream about creating my own fragrance brand and donating the profits to children in need.

Without a doubt, I have many new big dreams ahead, so I better go back to work. Some of them are still barely ideas, other are already works in progress in the pipeline. All I know is that when someone asks me, '*Is this your dream job you are working in?*', I would like to able to answer frankly, '*Yes*'. When someone asks me, '*Are you having the time of your life?*', I would like to answer '*I am*'. Moreover, I long for the possibility to make this happen for many other people, too.

After all, nothing is impossible – or so I have learned.

References and Suggested Books for Inspiration

Covey, S. R. (1989). *The 7 Habits of Highly Effective People.* New York: Free Press.

Hansson, J. F. (2010). *Rework.* New York: The Crown Publishing Group.

Hsieh, T. (2010). *Delivering Happiness.* New York: Business Plus.

Kahneman, D. (2011). *Thinking, Fast and Slow.* New York: Farrar, Straus and Giroux.

Kingsley, P. (2012). *How To Be Danish.* London: Short Books.

Klauser, H. A. (2000). *Write It Down, Make It Happen: Knowing What You Want And Getting It.* New York: Touchstone.

Robbins, A. (1992). *Awaken The Giant Within.* London: Simon & Schuster Ltd.

Schwartz, D. (1959). *The Magic of Thinking Big.* Los Angeles: Wilshire Book Co.

Webb, C. (2016). *How to Have a Good Day.* London: Pan Macmillan.

Wiking, M. (2016). *The Little Book of Hygge: The Danish Way to Live Well.* London: Penguin UK.

Acknowledgements

When I started this book in 2014, I had many doubts. I am not a native English speaker, and despite writing countless assignments during my university education, I had my English grammar insecurities. Despite this, every single sentence is this book, imperfect or not, has been written by me (I would never consider using a ghostwriter – I believe in the genuine, authentic writing and thoughts). Therefore, I would like to first and foremost thank my editors at Cornerstones for their invaluable feedback and suggestions. That helped me improve enormously and gave me more confidence in the English proficiency in the book.

I would like to thank my amazing boyfriend, best friend and the love of my life, who is mentioned quite a lot throughout the book – Jasen. I have no idea what I must have done in a previous life, if such exist, to deserve you! Thank you for everything! For loving my restlessness, and also for proof-reading this book several times – how you found the patience and time to do that is beyond me. Thank you, grande amore mio!

I would also like to thank all the amazing people, who, during my small research while writing this book, gave me their perspectives on living abroad. Your input was priceless, thank you so much!

Endless gratitude to Jane Midtgaard Madsen, Sandra Dorn, Stoyan Yankov, and Jakob Boman for their expert reviews of the book – your opinion and feedback meant a lot!

Thank you, amazing, talented Simona Ivanova (C'MNKY Art) for the beautiful illustrations you made for this book! Special gratitude also to one of my most favorite photographers in the whole world – Violeta (Villi) Pefticheva for capturing the front-cover!

Last, but not least, from the bottom of my heart, thank you, all you wonderful people, who have spent the time to read this book!

www.ingramcontent.com/pod-product-compliance
Lightning Source LLC
LaVergne TN
LVHW052100090426
835512LV00036B/2741